Teens Love and Want to F*ck James Franco:
A Study of a Life and Works

Mo Ibrahim

Lad Literature Books
New York

Published by Lad Literature Books
New York, NY
www.LadLiterature.com

ISBN: 9798566485218

FAIR USE ACT DISCLAIMER

Fair Use

Contents

Preface

In "Because", a poem in *Directing Herbert White: Poems*, Franco shared:

> And I holed up in my place and read my life away,
>
> And I watched a million movies, twice

And he further elaborated on his work ethic in "Nocturnal":

> I fight sleep like it's a sickness
>
> I work up my resistance.
>
> I push it back as far as possible
>
> Every night, like a runner,
>
> Working down his time,
>
> I run through books
>
> And hike through films
>
> And write like a sprinter.
>
> I'm a nocturnal creature,
>
> And I'm here to cheat time,
>
> You can see time and exhaustion
>
> Taking pay from my face-

During the summer of 2010, I taught a morning summer school class near the East Village. After school, I would typically go to an overpriced trendy fast food joint or *café* that I read about in *New York* magazine. After which, upon the Uptown 4, I would read Howard E. Gardner's *Creating Minds: An Anatomy of Creativity Seen*

Through the Lives of Freud, Einstein, Picasso, Stravinsky, Eliot, Graham, and Ghandi. And after reaching my walkup in The Bronx, I would continue working on my first novella.

In hindsight, Gardner prepared me to meet James Franco. Here's an excerpt from what Gardner wrote about Sigmund Freud:

> In his autobiographical study, Freud said: "[I] felt no particular partiality for the position and activity of a physician in those early years. . . .Rather I was moved by a sort of greed for knowledge." This comment is an understatement. In the eight years that passed between graduation from the gymnasium and receipt of the medical degree, Freud immersed himself spectacularly in the world of knowledge. He read extremely widely: the Bible, ancient classics, William Shakespeare in German and in English, Miguel de Cervantes, Molière, Gotthold Lessing, Johann Wolfgang von Goethe, and Friedrich von Schiller. He mastered English and French and also taught himself Spanish so that he could read Cervantes in the original. Fond of art and the theater, he attended many exhibitions and plays and commented penetratingly on what he had observed. Succumbing for a while to philosophy, he joined a society in which he read the major philosophers, translated John Stuart Mill into German, and took courses for three years with Franz Brentano, a respected philosopher at the University of Vienna with a special interest in psychological issues. And, not neglecting the area of science, he mastered [...] texts by the most

important scientist of the period, Hermann von Helmholtz.

Towards the end of the summer, while still on a high from Gardner's *Creating Minds*, the mailman delivered a fascinating *New York* magazine cover story on James Franco. Here are my highlights from Sam Anderson's article "Is James Franco For Real?":

1. He's just flown back from Berlin this afternoon, he says, and he has a 35-page paper due tomorrow. Next weekend he has to shoot a student film, because in two weeks he'll be flying out to Salt Lake City to start acting in a movie called *127 Hours*.

2. Revisions are due soon on his book of short stories, which will be published in October by Scribner. He's trying to nail down the details of an art show that will be based, somehow, on his recent performance on the soap opera *General Hospital*. Also, he has class every day, which—since he's enrolled in four graduate programs at once—requires commuting among Brooklyn, Greenwich Village, Morningside Heights, and occasionally North Carolina.

3. He persuaded his advisers [at UCLA] to let him exceed the maximum course load, then proceeded to take 62 credits a quarter, roughly three times the normal limit. When he had to work—to fly to San Francisco, for instance, to film *Milk*—he'd ask classmates to record lectures for him, then listen to them at night in his trailer. He graduated in two

years with a degree in English and a GPA over 3.5. He wrote a novel as his honors thesis.

4.   As soon as Franco finished at UCLA, he moved to New York and enrolled in four of them: NYU for filmmaking, Columbia for fiction writing, Brooklyn College for fiction writing, and—just for good measure—a low-residency poetry program at Warren Wilson College in North Carolina. This fall, at 32, before he's even done with all of these, he'll be starting at Yale, for a Ph.D. in English, and also at the Rhode Island School of Design.

5.   According to everyone I spoke with, Franco has an unusually high metabolism for productivity. He seems to suffer, or to benefit, from the opposite of ADHD: a superhuman ability to focus that allows him to shuttle quickly between projects and to read happily in the midst of chaos. He hates wasting time—a category that includes, for him, sleeping. (He'll get a few hours a night, then survive on catnaps, which he can fall into at any second, sometimes even in the middle of a conversation.) He doesn't drink or smoke or—despite his convincingness in *Pineapple Express*—do drugs. He's engineered his life so he can spend all his time either making or learning about art.

6.   Vince Jolivette, Franco's roommate and general right-hand man (he runs Franco's production company and plays bit parts in many of his films), met Franco in acting class in 1996. "Our teacher made us rehearse at least once a day outside of class," he told me. "James would get eight

or nine rehearsals. Everyone else would do, at most, one. If we didn't rehearse, or if I had to cancel, he'd be pissed."

7. According to his mother, Betsy, Franco has been this way since he was born. In kindergarten, he wouldn't just build regular little block towers—he'd build structures that used every single block in the playroom. At night, he would organize his Star Wars toys before he slept. When Franco was 4 years old, a friend of the family died. Betsy gave him the standard Mortality Talk: no longer with us, just a part of life—yes, but hopefully not for a very long time. Little James burst into tears. He was inconsolable. Eventually, he managed to choke out, between sobs, "But I don't want to die! I have so much to do!"

8. One of Franco's most serious productivity advantages is his personal assistant, Dana Morgan. "I tease him when people say, 'How do you do it?'" she tells me. "'You don't! You do all the things they know about, but you don't do the normal human-being things.'" Morgan [...] makes sure he wakes up, gets dressed, eats. "I guarantee you he would not eat unless I fed him."

Impressed by Franco's admirable work ethic, I started viewing and reading his works. For example, I viewed *The Dangerous Book Four Boys* art exhibit at the, now shuttered, Clocktower Gallery in Chinatown, and I read *Palo Alto*. With the exception of the short film *Dicknose in Paris* (2008), *The Dangerous Book Four Boys* was not, in my opinion, as intriguing as the nympholepsy and graphic teen sex in *Palo Alto*.

Subsequently, I read *Actors Anonymous* and *Directing Herbert White: Poems*, which were peppered with nympholepsy and teen sex as well. And I became a James Franco follower - on @JamesFrancoTV - his Instagram account, which exposed me to Franco's nymphet followers. Despite my years of research into nympholepsy and teleiophilia, I was a bit surprised to read comments posted on Franco's Instagram account such as "FUCK ME", "Daddy", "How young is too young?", and "15 year old dream come true?"

However, after the Franco's 2014 Instagram scandal, where 35-year-old Franco invited Lucy Clode, a 17-year-old fan, to his Manhattan hotel room, Franco deleted @JamesFrancoTV but not before I was able to publish the blog "Teens Love and Want to F*ck James Franco: James Franco's Instagram Archive". (Browse to www.TheWriterMoIbrahim.com for links to the Franco's Instagram archive.) As I maintained the blog, I continued to read and annotate Franco's works: Strongest of the Litter, A California Childhood, Hollywood Dreaming: Stories, Pictures, and Poems, and Straight James/Gay James - all of which contained nympholepsy and teen sex.

Like Franco's art, I am not a stan of his movies, but I found *Herbert White* (2010), Lifetime's *Mother, May I Sleep with Danger?* (2016) and *High School Lover* (2017) intriguing for the same reasons that I found his books to be provocative. Ergo, I decided to pen this book to share my analysis of @JamesFrancoTV's comments, where I found that teens love and want to "fuck" James Franco, and to explore the nympholepsy and teen sex in Franco's oeuvre.

Introduction

James Franco shared in his *New York Times* piece "The Meanings of the Selfie":

> The likes spin out of control for selfies of me [from my] legion of teenage fans.

> Attention is power. And if you are someone people are interested in, then the selfie provides something very powerful, from the most privileged perspective possible.

> We speak of the celebrity selfie, which is its own special thing. It has value regardless of the photo's quality, because it is ostensibly an intimate shot of someone whom the [often teen] public is curious about.

> [...] stars know the power of their image, and how it is enhanced when garnished with privileged material — anything that says, "Here is a bit of my private life."

But in the poem "New Rebel" from *Straight/James Gay James*, Franco wrote:

> I hate a selfie as much as anyone. But I love a selfie more than anyone. Know why? Because it's mine. And yours is yours. It is taken in that special place between self and mirror. If it's a true selfie it is held by the subject, so that the arm is circling out in front of the person, and the

camera is just an extension of the self. Like an octopus tentacle with an eye at the end looking back at its body."

[I was] [t]eaching graduate film at the best film schools in the country and posting shirtless selfies.

Oddly, Franco didn't write anything about the comments, very often from teens, that his selfies conjured. Here is a sampling of comments that were provoked by an Instagram selfie Franco posted from a plane to promote his appearance on the *Late Show with David Letterman*:

> Kyliee_0: you're so perfect!!! [heart emoji]
> kristinevalentine22: I wanna bang you so bad james
> quiroga_s: [...] I don't know why I want to fuck him
> aa706__: So sexy!
> kimyakiarash: daddy. [tongue emoji]

Interestingly, similar comments were posted on Franco's Instagram account by almost every race, ethnicity and major religion. For example, Latina Catholic teens were frequent commenters. And teens and young women offered almost every form of sex to Franco - including anal. Thereby, helping to dispel the myth that men are the primary architects of age-gap relationships when in fact, as Mary E. Odem related in *Delinquent Daughters,* teens and young women are often the aggressors. (However, it's the responsibility of men to avoid illegal age-gap relationships that may violate age of consent laws, because nymphets <u>never</u> go to jail for illicit intimate age-gap relationships.)

As an example, Odem related that during World War I, due to a rise in venereal diseases among soldiers, a five-mile moral zone, where alcohol and prostitution were prohibited, was established around military training camps. To the surprise of the military, it was discovered that it was not professional prostitutes who were loitering around military bases - it was thousands of teens.

And let it be known that the comments I archived from Franco's Instagram account are only samples. There were hundreds of similar raunchy comments, but Instagram's comments are dynamic (i.e., what is displayed changes as more comments are posted.) and it appears that the full list of comments can only be viewed by the owner of the account. Admittedly, all of the comments were not of a sexual nature. For instance, Franco was often praised for his artistic accomplishments.

Strikingly, (some) the teens in Franco's Instagram comments reminded me of the teens in Franco's books. For example, take *Palo Alto's* Pam, who, the summer between sophomore and junior year at Palo Alto High School, visited Simon Kat's house. The narrator of the short story described what happened after Roberto got Pam naked: "The guys lined up outside the bedroom. We went in, two and three at a time. Everyone fucked her. She got really messy." And Roberto described what he did to Pam: "I put a carrot in her butt. Everyone in the door was laughing [...] She let me keep it in there for a while. I moved it in and out. Then Jose and Angelo stopped, and we turned her over onto her back. I put a cucumber inside her. She didn't really want it, but I shoved it up there. I kept it up there for a while." Per Kim Potts of *Moviefone*, Franco did not want his mother to read *Palo Alto*. Now we know why.

But it was a bit difficult to keep up with all the raunchy teens in Franco's oeuvre, because Franco reused variations of the same writings in different texts. For example, Lindsay Lohan is littered throughout Franco's oeuvre, but in *Hollywood Dreaming: Stories, Pictures, and Poems*, she is "The Voice of Lindsay Lohan" but in *Directing Herbert White: Poems* the same poem is simply titled "Lindsay". A young "Elizabeth Taylor" is in *Strongest of the Litter* <u>and</u> *Hollywood Dreaming: Stories, Pictures, and Poems*. And "Seventh Grade", where there was "[...] a girl named Yvon that sucked Shaka's dick," is in *Strongest of the Litter* and *Directing Herbert White: Poems*.

In addition to nubile nymphets, Franco's books contained a number of references to nympholepsy in popular culture, which took me down a plethora of nympholepsy rabbit holes that may have been missed by the unsuspecting reader. For instance, there's a reference to *Fast Times at Ridgemont High* (1982) in *Palo Alto*. In *Palo Alto*, April had a sexual affair with Mr. B - her forty-two-year-old tanned 8th grade soccer coach. And in *Fast Times at Ridgemont High* (1982), Stacy, a 15-year-old high school sophomore, lost her virginity to Ron Johnson, a 26-year-old audio consultant - in a baseball dugout.

I focused on Franco's books, but I did cover a number of his films like Lifetime's *High School Lover* (2017) where a high school student performed oral sex on a 26-year-old A-list actor - in a helicopter. But covering Franco's films proved to be a bit difficult as well. For example, *Actors Anonymous* (2017) played in the 2017 Cinequest Film Festival, but it doesn't appear that the film was picked up for distribution; thus, I have no idea if the line: "Like eighteen […] Sheeeit, you think she's a virgin? […] Little slut, hungh?" was in the film. And as of fall of 2020, despite settling a copyright claim lawsuit, *Bukowski* (2013) was never released; thus, we may never know if the film contains any references to Bukowski's nympholepsy that is liberally peppered throughout his oeuvre.

This volume contains three (long) chapters: Nympholepsy in James Franco's Oeuvre, The Instagram Scandal, and The Daddy Thing.

Nympholepsy in James Franco's Oeuvre covers *Palo Alto* (2010), *Strongest of the Litter* (2012), *A California Childhood* (2013), *Actors Anonymous* (2013), *Hollywood Dreaming* (2014), *Directing Herbert White* (2014), *Straight James/Gay James* (2015), *Palo Alto* (2013) [film], *Mother, May I Sleep with Danger?* (2016) [Lifetime], *High School Lover* (2017) [Lifetime], *Pineapple Express* (2008) [film], *Herbert White* (2010) [short film] and *Spring Breakers* (2012) [film].

The Instagram Scandal covers Franco's 2014 Instagram scandal where it was revealed that he invited a Scottish nymphet to his Manhattan hotel room.

I went down a number of nympholepsy rabbit holes in the first two chapters, but The Daddy Thing chapter, which explores the "daddy thing" in popular culture, is a rabbit hole. It's worth noting that my *The Allure of Nymphets: From Emperor Augustus to*

Woody Allen, A Study of Man's Fascination with Very Young Women, the book and the blog, were heavily referenced for the rabbit holes.

And lastly, you may want to review these vocabulary words before delving into the chapters:

1. nymph·et /nimˈfet/ (noun): a sexually attractive girl or young woman. (Oxford Languages)

2. nym·pho·lep·sy /ˈnimfəˌlepsē/ (noun): passion aroused in men [i.e., nympholepts] by beautiful young girls. (Oxford Languages)

3. ephebophilia: the primary sexual interest [of an ephebophile] in mid-to-late adolescents, generally ages 15 to 19. ("Pedophilia, Hebephilia, and the DSM-V". *Archives of Sexual Behavior.*)

4. teleiophilia: a sexual preference [by teleiophiles] for adults. ("Fraternal birth order and sexual orientation in pedophiles". *Archives of Sexual Behavior.*)

5. pedophilia: 1. A sexual preference for pre-pubertal or early pubertal children. 2. For six months or more the person has acted on those urges or suffers from distress as a result of having the urges. 3. And the individual must be at least 16-years-old and at least five years older than the subject of desire. (*Are All Men Pedophiles?* (2013))

Chapter 1

Nympholepsy in James Franco's Oeuvre

Palo Alto: Stories (2010)

Here's part of Amazon's plot summary for James Franco's *Palo Alto: Stories,* which, per Potts, were: "[...] inspired by his teenage exploits.":

> James Franco's story collection traces the lives of a group of teenagers as they experiment with vices of all kinds, struggle with their families and one another, and succumb to self-destructive, often heartless nihilism.

And "vices of all kinds" is no hyperbole. Franco's short stories includes teen oral sex, teen sex, teen anal sex and teen orgies. And the stories include a number of age-gap sexual scenes and references.

Franco wrote in "Palo Alto Revisited: From Life to Book to Screen": "Some of the *Palo Alto* stories are based on experiences I had. Some are based on the experiences of other people, and others I made up." "I wanted the book to [...] be universal in the way it spoke about youth and about being human." And Franco wrote that the stories were inspired by "[....] voices from my youth [...]".

Alas, let's take a look at some of the teen "vices" in the Franco's stories:

"Lockheed"

In "Lockheed", during the summer between her freshman and sophomore years of high school, Marissa got a summer job recording "blemishes and splices" in "old film reels of the moon." However, Marissa got bored and drew: "[...] people getting shot and bleeding, and people having sex." Marissa shared that her life was boring too: "I only had one kiss, and it was with my gay cousin, Jamie." At a high school party, Marissa saw Zack Cuttle, a water polo player: "[...] getting a blowjob from someone behind the car."

In "Emily", Emily disclosed that Ryan wasn't: "[...] like the assholes in my grade like Adam and Roberto who just wanted to fuck and do it in the ass. Or come on my face like a porn star [...]" At a house party hosted by the Patten twins, Emily played I Never with the twins and a "bunch of other girls." Here are the rules of the game: "Someone says, "I never..." and if you've done the thing that they say [...] you have to drink."

"I never had sex at school."

I drank.

"I never had sex with two guys at once."

I drank.

"I never had sex with three guys at once."

Thus, we learned from the game that Emily had sex at school and that she was involved in a teen orgy.

After the game, Emily described what she did to Ryan in one of the twins' bedrooms: "[...] I told him to lie back and he did. His feet were on the floor. Then I undid his pants. I pulled his boxer shorts down to his feet. I did it for a while. He made sounds [...] After it was finished [...] I asked him if he liked it."

"Camp"

In "Camp", at the YMCA water-ski camp, some twelve and thirteen-year-old boys dared Howard to "make out" with Angela, a Black girl, in the back of the bus. Consequently, Howard kissed Angela, the other boys saw Howard feel Angela's "small breasts, and under the towel he felt her vagina."

In "Camp" is where we see our first example of nympholepsy. The narrator related that he had his first girlfriend in fourth grade - in Mr. DeFelice's class. "Her name was Simone. She was pretty and blonde like Madonna [...] Once Simone said Mr. DeFelice asked if he could take pictures of her at his house, but her mom wouldn't let her go."

Later, the narrator shared: "The second time [I had sex] was in Susan's bed. I was about to come [...] After, when we pulled away, it was sticky and frothy. Buttery, like pulling apart a Baby Ruth."

"Chinatown In Three Parts" is about Pam, a half Vietnamese and half Caucasian teen, who Roberto, the 16-year-old narrator, met in Jordan Middle School's parking lot.

In "Part 1: Vietnam", after smoking "a lot of pot" at Tom's house, Roberto suggested to Pam, "Let's play 'Camping'!" Roberto detailed what he did to Pam during Camping: "[...] I took her pants off. [...] Her ass was fantastic, very hard. And her tits were big for an Asian. I spit on my hand, and then I put my dick inside her. It was good [...]"

In "Part II: Headless", Pam gave Roberto a "blowjob" in the shed behind her home. "I asked her if she liked it. She said that she did. Then I left."

A week later, Pam: "[...] on her knees in the middle of the soft, manicured [lawn] bowling green [...]", had an (oral sex) orgy with Seth, Tom and Roberto.

Roberto described his turn: "After, Tom zipped up [...] She stayed on her knees. Next, I walked over to her, before Seth, because I didn't want her to be too messy. She had to do it for a while. I made a mess. It got on her shirt and hair. I laughed, and Tom laughed. She was all messy for Seth."

The following summer, between her sophomore and junior year of high school, Pam visited Simon Kats' house. Conveniently: "His mom worked nights as a nurse." On one occasion, Roberto got Pam naked before: "The guys lined up outside the bedroom. We went in, two and three at a time. Everyone fucked her. She got really messy."

Roberto described what he did to Pam: "I put a carrot in her butt. Everyone in the door was laughing [...] She let me keep it in there for a while. I moved it in and out. Then Jose and Angelo stopped, and we turned her over onto her back. I put a cucumber inside her. She didn't really want it, but I shoved it up there. I kept it up there for a while."

In "Part III: Caffe Buon", Al, an Italian bartender at Caffee Buon, told Roberto that if he got him "laid", Roberto could have a free dinner. Consequently, at five o'clock on a Monday, Roberto took Pam to restaurant where Al, who is also a friend of Roberto's dad, had sex in the bathroom while Roberto dined on "a chicken dinner with farfalle". Subsequently, Roberto took Pam back to Caffee Buon. While Roberto lunched on angel hair pasta with shrimp, Juan, a cook, and Pam, a (high school) student, had sex in the kitchen's bathroom.

Next, Franco returned from age-gap sex to teen sex. In the parking lot behind Palo Alto High School: "She [Pam] got into the back seat. She was on her hands and knees on the seat. Seth got behind her [...] He pushed her skirt up and took off her panties. Ramone stood at the open back door, in front of her face, and undid his pants. His dick was huge [...] Seth was doing it really hard, and the car was shaking. Pam was choking [...]"

In "Part III: April" of the short story "April In Three Parts", April attended a bat mitzvah where Shauna became a "woman". But before going to the bat mitzvah, April went to Mr. B's house to babysit Michael - Mr. B's five-year-old son. April and Michael watched *Fast Times at Ridgemont High*, which April described as: "[Teen] [s]ex in a baseball dugout, [teen] sex in a pool, and abortion."

After Mr. B returned from his date with another teacher, April put on a "light lavender" dress. Before driving April to the bat mitzvah and giving her a kiss on the cheek, Mr. B informed April, "I really fucking like you, April." April replied, "I like you too."

After losing at the soccer championships that were held at a junior high school in Los Altos, Mr. B drove April to his house. April described what happened: "We went to the couch. I was wearing sweats and he undressed me and got a condom and I lay on my back and we did it, simple. And then it was over. I was fourteen." And Mr. B was 42.

Mr. B, whom April additionally described as having "[...] a good body, good hair, and a nice smile", and April maintained their teacher-student affair for almost two years. The affair even continued after April started high school at Paly. The only person who knew about the affair was April's sister who opined that affair was "okay" as long as Mr. B and April were in love.

But before moving on to the next short story where we learn more about April, let's go down our first nympholepsy rabbit hole and elaborate on April's description of *Fast Times at Ridgemont High*.

Per IMDb, *Fast Times at Ridgemont High* (1982) is about: "A group of Southern California high school students [...] enjoying their most important subjects: sex, drugs, and rock n' roll." The film doesn't have a lot of rock n' roll, it does contain some drugs, but there's a lot of [teen] sex. And two age-gap relationships.

Four minutes into the teen comedy, the following conversation took place at a pizza parlor in the Ridgemont Mall between Stacy, a 15-year-old high school sophomore, and Ron Johnson, a 26-year-old audio consultant:

> Ron Johnson: "You look like you could still be in high
> School."
> Stacy: "Yeah, I know. Everybody says that."
> Ron Johnson: "How old are you?"
> Stacy: "19. How old are you?"
> Ron Johnson: "26. Do you think we could still
> be friends?"
> Stacy: "So what can I get for you?"
> Ron Johnson: "How about a meatball sandwich, a
> medium Coke, and your phone number?"

After work, Stacy shared with Linda, her co-worker and schoolmate, that Ron gave her his business card, but that she was hesitant about giving him a call. Linda adjured Stacy to call Ron, and Linda shared with Stacy that she had sex when she 13 and that it was no big deal because, "It's just sex." (By the way, Linda was having her own an age-gap affair with Doug whom Linda described as, "[...] no high school boy.")

> Linda: "Why don't you call him?"
> Stacy: "I can't."
> Linda: "Yes, you can. Guys love that sort of thing."
> Stacy: "Really?"
> Linda: "Yes. Stacy, what are you waiting for? You're 15-years-old. I did it when I was 13. It's no huge thing. It's just sex."

During lunch in Ridgemont High's cafeteria, Linda was flabbergasted to learn that Stacy didn't know how to give a blowjob. Consequently, to the delight of the high school boys, Linda taught Stacy how to perform fellatio on a carrot.

Linda, "You've never given a blowjob? Never? Stace, there's nothing to it. It's so easy. Relax your throat muscles. Don't bite. And slide it in. Good. Push it slowly in and out. You got it!"

After taking Linda's advice to call Ron, Stacy had a *rendez-vous* with the audio consultant. Consequently, Ron drove Stacy to a baseball field and took her virginity in the dugout after he asked, "Are you really 19?" Stacy lied, "Yeah, yeah I am. I'm really 19." (Note: IRL, if it came out that Ron and Stacy had had (consensual) sex, despite Stacy's repeated lie, poor Ron wouldn't have had a chance in a court of law, Stacy wouldn't have a chance of being reprimanded, Linda would have probably testified against poor Ron, and Ron would have been, incorrectly, referred to as an pedophile instead of as an ephebophile.)

In school, Stacy told Linda, "[...] it hurt so bad." To which Linda consoled, "Don't worry. Keep doing it. It gets a lot better. I swear."

Interestingly, Amy Heckerling, the film's director, made full use of the allure of nymphets by showing both the Stacy and Linda topless.

Per Wikipedia, *Fast Times at Ridgemont High* was selected for preservation in the United States National Film Registry by the Library of Congress as being "culturally, historically, or aesthetically significant". The film cost $5 million to make, but it made $50 million. The film is based on Cameron Crowe's book *Fast Times at Ridgemont High: A True Story*. And most recently, a Zoom table read of the film was performed to support the Community Organized Relief Effort's COVID-19. The table read was introduced by Eric Garcetti - the Mayor of Los Angeles. Jennifer Aniston played Linda and Julia Roberts played Stacey.

"Tar Baby" elaborates a bit on April. We learn that April moved to Palo Alto: "[...] at thirteen with her tan and muscular legs, [and that] she had already fucked [before having sex with Mr. B]." In addition, after April started high school, she started: "[...] fucking older guys. This guy Denny Johnson and this guy Adam Cohen. They played water polo, and were really tall. Also my friend Barry."

Towards the end of "Tar Baby", Teddy, the narrator: "[...] started thinking about Jack Kerouac and what a hero he was," which reminded me of Kerouac's *On The Road*, where Dean (Neal Cassady) reminisced about a three-day liaison in the Ace Hotel with fifteen-year-old Marylou, whom he described as, "[...] so sweet then, so young, hmm, ahh!" And Teddy imparted that he: "[...] read Ibsen's *Ghosts* in the parking lot one day while waiting for an AA meeting because the court made me go." Teddy must be a fast reader, because it took me almost three hours to read *Ghosts,* which is about Regina Engstrand, a young maid, who was the illegitimate daughter, via Joanna, a young maid, of Captain Alving. Regina was <u>wanted</u> by her stepfather and older brother. Ibsen didn't provide the ages of Joanna and Regina, but they were both described as young and Regina was further described as, "Isn't she splendid to look at? What a figure! And the picture of health!" A, "[...] fine, splendid, [and] handsome girl [...]" And Regina described herself as, "A poor girl [who] must make some use of her youth [...]"

Lastly, in "I Could Kill Someone", "[...] in eighth grade Teague took Kate ["Keller, who went to the all-girls school, Castilleja."] to *Wayne's World* and fingered her during the whole movie. Just watching and working."

Interestingly, *O, The Oprah Magazine*, opined of *Palo Alto: Stories*: "Spare and riveting." I'm not sure what spare means in this context, but *The Economist* opined: "Startling and original." And *Vogue* concluded: "Compelling and gutsy." Gia Coppola must have agreed with Oprah, because she wrote and directed *Palo Alto* (2013) while Franco's Rabbit Bandini was the film's production company.

IMDb posted a brief plot summary for *Palo Alto* (2013): "The life and struggles of a group of adolescents living in Palo Alto." No worries. We'll provide some details. Coppola relied heavily on Franco's short stories for the dialogue but, taking advantage of the allure of nymphets, she took some liberties with some of the scenes.

In the opening scene, Fred asked Teddy what he would do if he could go back in time. Teddy replied that he would be a king, "And I'd fuck every virgin in the kingdom." Interestingly, this reminded me of Augustus, the first emperor of the Roman Empire, who Matt Ridley related in the *New York Times* Notable Book *The Red Queen: Sex and the Evolution of Human Nature* had "a passion for deflowering girls" and according to Roman historian Suetonius, the virgins were procured by Augustus' wife.

A little over a minute later, the following conversation took place among stretching coed soccer players:

Chrissy: "Oh, I'm so wet. Not in a good way, either. Mr. B's [her high school teacher and soccer coach] a hottie though."

Shauna: "Fuck, I know. Too bad he wants to get in with April."

Chrissy: "I'd go for it if I were you."

April: "Guys, that's so awkward. I babysit his kid."

Shauna: "So?"

Chrissy wagered: "I bet he makes a really ugly face when he comes."

In one of her first deviations from the book and taking advantage of the allure of nymphets, at the 7:16 mark in the film, Coppola decided to have April dance on a bed in a satin mini chemise. April bounced upon the bed seductively while she raised her mini slip and lowered a strap to fully expose her bra.

Like in the book, the teens played Never Have I Ever, but in the book, the game revealed that Emily had sex at school and that she participated in a teen orgy. However, in the film, Shauna described how to play Never Have I Ever:

"You just say, "Never Have I Ever and then if you've done the thing you have to drink [...] Um, Never Have I Ever given Seth Monkarsh a blowjob during free period in the senior parking lot."

"Drink up, Chrissy."

After Chrissy drank, she said, "Okay fine, my turn. Um, hmm. Never Have I Ever kissed my uncle," to which Shauna said slyly before she drank from her red plastic cup, "Are you fucking serious? That was private."

In addition, the game revealed that Chrissy participated in a teen "lesbianic experience". But Chrissy's blowjob in the senior parking lot, her teen lipstick lesbian "experience", and Shauna's kiss with her uncle were not in the book. Why did Coppola add those to the film? (That's a rhetorical question.)

However, in the book and the film, Emily gave Teddy a blowjob in the bedroom of Shauna's parents. Poolside the next day, Chrissy said, "Emily blew Teddy last night in your parent's bedroom." To which Shauna replied, "She will suck any dick that anyone puts in her face." (To clarify, Teddy didn't put his dick in Emily's face. Emily put Teddy's dick in her face.")

In another interesting deviation from the book, "Cock 4 dayz" was "written" in preschool magnetic letters on an appliance in Shauna's house. Why?

While babysitting, April said to Michael - Mr. B's son, "Come on, enough of this [video] game. Let's watch a movie." Michael said, "I don't think I'm allowed to watch this movie [i.e., *Fast Times at Ridgemont High*]." Subsequently, a topless teen on the screen elicited a "Whao" from the elementary school aged Michael. After another babysitting session, Mr. B (James Franco) kissed April (Emma Roberts).

"I really like you." Mr. B confessed.

"I really like you." April confessed.

"Yeah but, I'm older and I know that there aren't a lot of good things around, and I know you are really good." Mr. B said to which April responded by returning his kiss.

In another scene that wasn't in the book, Coppola directed Fred to push Emily down by the shoulders and demand, "Tell me you love me," before Emily gave him a blowjob in her parent's backyard.

However, the following voice-over from that scene is from the book:

> Emily didn't have any friends [...] The only person she knew was me [...] One afternoon we went to Jason King's house [...] Jason's parents were gone [...] We were drinking sodas and vodka and smoking pot. [...] I got her into Jason's parents' bed and got her naked. The guys lined up outside the bedroom door. [...] We went in two or three at a time. Everyone fucked her [...] She gave me a blowjob. I asked if she liked it. She said she did [...]

Back at Mr. B's house, the following conversation took place:

> April: "Why don't you talk to me at school anymore?"
> Mr. B: "You know why."
> April: "Yeah, but you can at least be nice to me and not ignore me. I mean, it's like you don't even like me anymore."
> Mr. B, committing an age-gap relationship *faux pas*, replied: "Are you kidding me. April I love you."
> April, perplexed: "What? That doesn't even make sense [...] I have to go."

Mr. B reiterated: "April I love you [...] You can say you're babysitting all the time and come over."

April: "I should be hanging out with boys my own age."

Mr. B: "Why? Why do you wanna hang out with a bunch of little boys? You're better than that. Just be with me."

But it was no use. April left.

In the bathroom between classes, Shauna complimented Chrissy, "Your tits are seriously huge today!" Chrissy, "I know, right?" Shauna, "They look amazing." But that dialogue was not in the book. I would love to know Coppola's inspiration.

After losing the soccer game, Mr. B consoled a crying Raquel (Margaret Qualley). "Consequently, April said, "Raquel is such a cry baby [...] I mean, do you even think she's pretty." Shauna opined, "Raquel? Yeah, she's fucking gorgeous."

Despite their previous conversation ending on a sour note, April went back to Mr. B's where they had sex on her high school teacher's sofa. And unlike in the book, Coppola choose to zoom in on April's panties that had the word Thursday printed across the front; thereby, reminding the viewers that April was an adolescent.

Subsequently, after Michael beat April in a Mortal Kombat match, he said, "I get two cookies, because I won."

"Says who?"

"Raquel (Margaret Qualley)."

"Raquel?"

"Raquel's my other babysitter [...]"

Interestingly, the book inferred that Mr. B and Raquel had an age-gap affair, but the film made it apparent. Mr. B pleaded, "Look, what happened between me and Raquel, it's nothing, okay? [...] You broke up with me. And we weren't talking to each other. Can I see you?"

April replied, "No. No, I'm not coming over there anymore." But did April keep her word?

Tom Shone of *The Guardian* gave *Palo Alto* (2013) 3 out of 5 stars and opined that Coppola had an "eye for cool composition". And in "Palo Alto Revisited: From Life to Book to Screen", Franco divulged his reasoning for hiring Coppola to direct *Palo Alto*: "I knew I wanted someone who shared my sensibility but could also take the material to new places." "She is a master of creating layers of meaning and feeling, ambiguous energy that elevates the subject from teenage drama into art." Aha! So, that's why Coppola choose to have Fred push Emily down by the shoulders and demand, "Tell me you love me," before Emily gave him a blowjob in her parent's backyard. That's why Shauna complimented Chrissy, "Your tits are seriously huge today!" And that's why Coppola elected to zoom in on April's panties that had the word Thursday printed across the front.

In an interview with Howard Stern, Franco shared that Mr. B was based on a junior high school teacher-student affair between a, "[…] 13, 14-year-old girl and a man in his forties." And towards the end of *Hollywood Dreaming: Stories, Pictures, and Poems,* Franco elaborated on Mr. B's backstory. During a Q&A after the screening of *Palo Alto* at the Cameo Cinema, Franco related to the moviegoers, which included Francis Ford Coppola:

> In *Palo Alto*, I play Mr. B, a character based on a real teacher who had a relationship with a girl in my class when we were in eighth grade [...] The real Mr. B was "Mr. Cool," but in a cheesy way. He coached girls' sports. And one time, when I was mad at him, I wrote Eighth Grade Girl Molester on his door placard [...] The girl, "April" in my book and the movie, would babysit his kid; she never told anyone that she was having sex with him at age thirteen while he was at least forty-three (echoes of Nicholas Ray and Natalie Wood's relationship - weird how it's more palatable for film people [i.e., celebrities] to statutory-rape).

In general, Franco's correct to assert that statutory rape committed by celebrities is more palatable to the public. For example, in addition to his relationship with Priscilla, that began when Priscilla was 14, Elvis <u>had</u> other nymphets. For instance, per Alanna Nash's *Baby, Let's Play House: Elvis Presley and the Women Who Loved Him*, after Elvis left the military, he began a six-year relationship with Sandy Ferra, which began when she was 14-years-old. However, Elvis frequently spoke to Priscilla on the phone while she remained in Germany. But once Priscilla arrived at Graceland, Elvis would have her dress up as a schoolgirl and videotape her having lipstick lesbian sex with another nymphet. And two years before his death, Elvis began a relationship with 14-year-old Reeca Smith. But the question is, have you ever heard anyone (incorrectly) accuse Elvis of being a pedophile?

In 1977, the Academy Award nominated film director Roman Polanski gave drugs to thirteen-year-old Samantha Geimer before he raped and sodomized her. According to *The Hollywood Reporter*, the rape occurred three weeks after Polanski took topless photos of the nymphet at her home in Los Angeles. It is widely believed that Polanski fled the United States to France to avoid going to jail and that he has avoided extradition by not visiting any countries that may be sympathetic to the United States; however, a summary of James Fox's 'Roman 'Holiday'" feature *Vanity Fair* will shed light on the matter:

> Despite feeling that it was consensual and that Geimer was responsive, Polanski pleaded guilty to having unlawful sex with a minor and for his punishment he was sent to a California institution by Judge Laurence J. Rittenband for a 90-day evaluation. Forty-two days later, Polanski's psychiatric report recommended that he be released with time served; therefore, contrary to popular belief, Polanski did not flee the country to escape imprisonment. He fled the country after he confessed, he was evaluated, and was released. That was enough for Geimer's family to drop the charges of lewd and lascivious acts upon a child under fourteen, rape by use of drugs, perversion, and sodomy – among other charges.

As a matter of fact, Geimer stated to director Marina Zenovich for her documentary *Roman Polanski: Odd Man Out* (2012) that Polanski was not a "molester", "pedophile" or "child rapist." And despite the fact that Polanski drugged and sodomized her when she was thirteen, Geimer stated on an episode of *Good Morning America* that the judges and district attorneys, "[…] caused way more damage to me and my family than anything Roman Polanski has ever done."

Now back to Franco's *Palo Alto* Q&A where Franco related his justification for writing about April's consensual yet illegal (in California) affair with Mr. B story:

> I put a version of the story in my book, even though it wasn't *my* story, because I felt it was important to talk about as it is something terrible that will continue to happen forever, and if put in the book at least people can be reminded of it, and maybe some young people won't feel as alone because they read something they could identify with.

In addition, Franco shared in *A California Childhood*, along with a photograph of the real Mr. B reclining upon a chair, his rationale for writing about the Palo Alto's teens and why he chose to "[...] use childhood, teenagers, and school as forms.":

> I use childhood, teenagers, and school as forms. For me the particulars of the time and place of my childhood are placeholders for anyone's experience at that age. In my work, I show a more troubled side of young people in Palo

Alto, not because I think the teenagers there are particularly bad, or because I think they are hard-off - far from it. I want to use them because I believe that all young people can be studied to access something more universal.

In addition, Franco related that Palo Alto is one of the wealthiest areas in the United States (e.g., Steve Job's daughter was in Franco's high school graduating class.). And by writing about wealthy nymphets of Palo Alto, Franco, like *Rebel Without a Cause's* Nicholas Ray, was able to compassionately prevent the teen's raunchy behavior from being: "[...] explained away by economic considerations, as could be done with troubled-youth films set in inner cities."

However, if we're ~~naive~~ courteous and accept that Franco was being truthful about sharing the raunchy exploits of affluent Palo Alto teens for altruistic reasons, I suspect that, additionally, Franco leaked their stories for the same reason *Law & Order: SVU* has been benefitting from the allure of nymphets by showing teen prostitutes, teen age-gap relationships, and statutory rape as entertainment for 21 seasons. Takis Würger summed it up well in her *New York Times* book review "In This Novel, a Secret Society Is Keeping Some Very Dark Secrets":

> The television show "Law & Order: SVU" is a good example. Its characters teem with righteous outrage and constantly pontificate and philosophize, creating a moral backdrop that lets viewers partake of the show's gruesome subject matter without feeling dirty.

Per Amazon: "There is a vision of power at the center of James Franco's first chapbook of poems, *Strongest of the Litter*." Vison of power? In the poem "Elizabeth Taylor", which is also in *Hollywood Dreaming: Stories, Pictures, and Poems*, Franco made a reference to Liz in *A Place in the Sun* (1951) by describing her as: "So young and natural".

We'll elaborate on *A Place in the Sun* (1951) when we discuss *Hollywood Dreaming*, but let's elaborate on Franco referring to Liz as "So young and natural," which brings to mind Tom Leonard's *The Daily Mail* post "This is Liz Taylor at 16. Had she ALREADY been seduced by half of Hollywood?" where Leonard wrote that Richard A. Lertzman and William J. Birnes related in *The Life and Times of Mickey Rooney* that Betty Jane, the pregnant second wife of 24-year-old Mickey Rooney, caught 12-year-old Elizabeth Taylor performing oral sex on Rooney in a dressing room on the Hollywood set of *National Velvet* (1944). Unsurprisingly, Jane was awarded a large settlement after the divorce.

And Darwin Porter and Danforth Prince alleged in *Elizabeth Taylor: There is Nothing Like a Dame* that 11-year-old Taylor was taught by *Lassie Come Home* star, Roddy McDowall, how to pleasure men sans copulation. Ultimately, 15-year-old Taylor lost her virginity to 24-year-old British actor Peter Lawford in a limousine on the way to the home of William Randolph Hearst.

J.D. Salinger stated after he met 15-year-old Taylor, "She is the most beautiful creature I have ever seen in my life." 38-year-old Robert Taylor adjured the camera men on the set of *Conspirator*

(1949) not to film his lower body while shooting a kissing scene with 16-year-old Taylor. And this was Orson Welles' reaction after he saw the "unbelievable" 15-year-old Taylor in the MGM commissary, "Unlike other figures in Hollywood, I have never found myself attracted to young girls. But Elizabeth Taylor had something which transcended age. I will never forget how she moved down the commissary aisle, holding her food tray. I lusted for that young girl and felt, for the first time in my life, like a dirty old man." Taylor stated that, allegedly, Welles eventually forced himself upon her in his dressing room.

But Taylor stated that she somewhat forced herself upon Ronald Reagan on the Hollywood sofa of the 36-year-old future president. Taylor related, "Reagan was treating me like a grown woman, and that thrilled me. We sat on his sofa and I could tell he wanted to get it on but he seemed reluctant to make the first move [so] I became the aggressor." Also, Taylor allegedly had a swimming pool threesome with her *A Date with Judy* (1948) co-star Robert Stack and congressman John F. Kennedy. Lastly, 15-year-old Taylor stated in a radio interview that she was "bored" by boys but, "wanted to do crazy, silly things [with] men." Like Franco wrote: "So young and natural"

In "Art School", Franco addressed helping "kids" turn their young passion into great art. And he noted his thirst, like a vampire, for the energy of the young:

> There is nothing like the energy
> Of the young. I thirst for it
> Like a vampire. I use young people
> Like they're oranges I'm squeezing.

In "De Niro", Franco named-dropped Travis Bickle:

> Travis Bickle and Jake LaMotta
> Have such defined edges
> They are sculptures
> Mysterious as Michelangelo's David.

Consequently, I would be remiss not to mention Travis' attempt to rescue Iris where in *Taxi Driver* (1976), Travis (Robert De Niro), a New York City taxi driver, desired to save Iris (Jodie Foster), a pre-teen prostitute, from her abusive pimp.

On Travis' first attempt at rescuing Iris, her pimp, dressed in black slacks, a white wife beater, and a matching black and white oversized fedora, gave Travis the rates and what it entailed:

> $15 - fifteen minutes, $25 - half-an-hour [...] Well, take it or leave it. If you want to save yourself some money, don't fuck her. 'Cause you'll be back here every night for some more man. She's 12-and-a-half years old [...] You ain't

never had no pussy like that. You can do anything you
want with her. You can cum on her. Fuck her in the
mouth. Fuck her in the ass. Cum on her face man. She'll
get your cock so hard; she'll make it explode. But no rough
stuff."

Interestingly, in one scene, while Travis was driving through the
seedy 1970s Times Square area, a theater's marquee sign advertised
the film *Anita: Swedish Nymphet* (1973), which is about a sixteen-
year-old nymphomaniac who satisfied her sexual urges with (older)
men.

In *A California Childhood,* Franco heartwarmingly wrote in the poem "Second Grade" that he had his first love in second grade:

> I fell in love for the first time.
> Jenny Brown.

And the two young love birds kissed:

> Jenny came over,
> Our mothers were friends
> And when the mothers left the room
> We kissed.

Franco didn't clarify, but I'm going to assume that that was Franco's first kiss. I would imagine that most would respond favorably to Franco's early loving kiss as "cute" but early voyeurism may elicit some different responses:

> Another time Jenny came over,
> And I propped open the bathroom window,
> And watched as she crouched
> Girl-like on the toilet.

In "My Place", Franco wrote about students doing "it" in a faculty bathroom:

> There is a faculty bathroom in the office building
> -Called the Tower Building-

The one-unit bathroom is for staff only,

But students sneak in there and do it.

Some of the short stories like "Camp" where, at the YMCA water-ski camp, Howard kissed Angela, felt her "small breasts, and under the towel he felt her vagina," are in *A California Childhood* as well. Thus, we'll flip over to "The Dear" in which Franco wrote: "I always sat in the back of Mr. Kim's algebra class. He was very enthusiastic about algebra. I drew a picture of me sticking my dick into Rex's blond dream girl."

The line: "[...] we watched a movie *Less Than Zero*. It was bad. Rex said that he read the book and it was better," took me down yet a nympholepsy rabbit hole.

I came upon Bret Easton Ellis' *Less Than Zero* while perusing the 2017 summer reading list of a Manhattan high school. The school is located in the Riffs' old neighborhood near the Drummond's street. Over a third of the students are white, 15% are Asian and according to *Great Schools*: "This school is rated above average in school quality compared to other schools in the state." The school is what I would call a public\private school since only 10% of the African American applicants were admitted.

Understandably, *Less Than Zero's* selection on the summer reading list warranted a teacher's disclaimer: "Note that this novel contains some disturbing content, including rape and drug use." But that was an understatement, because the teacher should have written "rapes" as there were not one, not two, not three but four nymphets who were raped in the novel.

In *Less Than Zero,* 18-year-old Clay, the novel's protagonist, while on winter break from his east coast college, attended a party in Malibu where:

> Everyone in the room is looking up at a large television screen [...] There's a young girl, nude, maybe fifteen, on a bed, her arms are tied together above her head and her legs spread apart, each foot tied to a bedpost [...] The camera cuts quickly to [...] this fat black guy, who's also naked and who's got this huge hardon [...] he has sex with the girl and then walks off the screen.

It was a snuff film, but the partygoers debated about whether or not the Black man actually killed the nymphet with "[…] an ice pick, and what looks like a wire hanger and a package of nails and then a thin, large knife […]"

After Clay visited Daniel's house, Daniel told Clay about a girl he knew but he didn't share her name:

> "She's pretty and sixteen and [...] she goes to Westward Ho on Westwood Boulevard and she meets her dealer there [...] And this guy spends all day shooting her full of smack again and again..."
>
> "And then he feeds her some acid and takes her off to a party in the hills or in the Colony and then...and then..." Daniel stops.
>
> "And then what?" I ask, handing him back the joint.
>
> "And then she gets gangbanged by the entire party."

Subsequently, Clay described a visit:

[...] to Rip's apartment in Wilshire, he leads us into the
bedroom. There's a naked girl, really young and pretty,
lying on the mattress. Her legs are spread and tied to the
bedposts and her arms are tied above her head. Her cunt
is all rashed and looks dry and I can see that it's been
shaved. She keeps moaning and murmuring words and
moving her head from side to side [...]
Rip says something.
"She's twelve."
"And she is tight, man," Spin laughs.
"Her name is Shandra and she goes to Corvalis
[Elementary School]" is all Rips says.

Clay declined to have sex with the nymphet but later shared:

A young girl from San Diego who had been at the party
[in Palm Springs on the desert with kids from L.A. and San
Francisco and Sacramento] had been found the next
morning, her wrists and ankles tied together. She had been
raped repeatedly. She also had been strangled and her
throat had been slit and her breasts had been cut off and
someone had stuck candles where they used to be. Her
body had been found at the Sun Air Drive-In hanging
upside down from the swing set [...]

Interestingly, Clay's blond younger sisters (approximately 13 and 15) enjoyed listening to "Teenage Enema Nurses in Bondage" by Killer Pussy, the youngest sister did cocaine, but both sisters watched porn (with the sound off), but, for some reason, one of the nymphets hated: "[…] it when they show the guy coming."

Here's an excerpt from the lyrics to "Teenage Enema Nurses in Bondage":

> Teenage, green age, awkward in-between age
> (Teenage enema nurse)
> I turned fifteen, thought it was a teen scene
> (Teenage enema nurse)
> Thought it would be easy, but it makes me queasy
> I'm a teenage enema nurse
>
> They told me, "Stick the nozzle in
> There's really nothing to it
> It's not a very pretty job
> But someone's got to do it

Danny Bonaduce, a former child actor on *The Partridge Family*, wrote in *Random Acts of Badness*, his autobiography, that the high school in *Less Than* Zero reminded him of The Buckley School, which is a high school in Sherman Oaks, California that he attended with a number of other celebrity students. Bonaduce wrote: "When the book *Less Than Zero* came out, all my classmates were pissed. Not because it was an exact portrayal of our school – but because we failed to get any royalties."

As you know, I'm a fan of Franco's work ethic; thus, I enjoyed reading about Teddy in "Friend of the Devil" who worked at a golf course driving the caged cart that retrieved the golf balls. To alleviate the monotony: "Teddy would hold books below the steering wheel and read while he picked up the balls. He loved Kerouac's *On the Road* [...]" where, like I wrote earlier, Dean (Neal Cassady) reminisced about a three-day liaison in the Ace Hotel with fifteen-year-old Marylou. And when Teddy wasn't efficiently multi-tasking:

> Teddy thought of girls. He thought of their vaginas and mouths and tits. He thought of blowjobs [...] and drunk girls, and cum on faces, and swallowing, and sitting on toilets, and naked bodies, and saliva [...] and his calculus teacher's ass shaking when she wrote on the chalkboard. And Erin who gave blowjobs in the art building bathroom [...]

In "Memoria", which is the last story in "A California Childhood", we learned that the girls in Mr. Moore's physics class opined that Mr. Moore's was handsome. And in creative writing class, Mr. Shotts read a student's creative writing: "[...] about a guy and a girl having sex in a car at Foothills Park." It turned out that IRL, the girl having sex in the car was Rahma who the students called: "[...] "Corn-the-Rahm" or "Rahma-mama," because Pete Eubanks stuck his thumb up her butt in a hot tub."

How about another Palo Alto teen orgy? In a bedroom in the "Guesthouse", which is the guesthouse where Byron lived behind his grandmother's house, four guys stood around the bed upon which was Natasha Illiichev was being, shall we say, being made love to by Jamie Berkof - "a big football player". Berkof "did it really hard", which caused Natasha's mouth to wobble open and her head to hit the wall. The narrator did not participate in the high school orgy, but upon returning home, he masturbated while thinking about Natasha's: "[...] moist tongue in her mouth, like a little animal. Like a little heart, being rocked back and forth." Tongue fetish?

In a *Daily Mail* article, "James Franco's Creepy Musings on Sex with 'Young Girls'.", Keith Griffith attempted to use Franco's *Actors Anonymous: A Novel* against him by referring to the novel as creepy for sentences like 'I have girls all over the world'. Let us take a look at the novel and you can determine if you agree or disagree with Griffith.

By page 43, the protagonist took an acting class on Lankershim Boulevard in LA where he participated in an improvisation scene from Mamet's *Sexual Perversity in Chicago*. In the scene, an 18-year-old little slut, with tits like melons, and ass like butter, candy, and an onion that would bring a tear to the eye, was described.

> "So, last night, how'd it go? […] "Don't bullshit," he said.
>
> "No bullshit."
>
> "So tell me. And no bullshit."
>
> "So tits like melons, no bullshit."
>
> "No shit?"
>
> "No shit, and an ass – momma."
>
> "A momma ass?"
>
> "No, an ass like butter. An ass like candy."
>
> "An ass like that?
>
> "An ass like an onion, bring a tear to your eye."
>
> "Like…"
>
> "Like eighteen […] Sheeeit, you think she's a virgin? […] Little slut, hungh?"

Franco wrote on page 51 that it's usually no fun to be the actor, director and writer of a film unless you're Charlie Chaplin or Woody Allen.

Joyce Milton related in her book, *Tramp: The Life of Charlie Chaplin*, that Chaplin acknowledged: "I had a violent crush on a girl only ten or twelve. I have always been in love with young girls [...]" In addition, Milton clarified that Chaplin developed a crush on 12-year-old Maybelle Fournier, he met Mildred Harris when she was 14-years-old and impregnated her when she was 16. Furthermore, Chaplin was smitten with 15-year-old Hetty Kelly, and he impregnated Lillita Grey when she was 15 - allegedly *before* they were married.

Speaking of Lillita Grey, when the actress was 12-years-old, she played a "flirtatious ang_l" in Chaplin's *The Kid* (1921). In the film, Lillita's character was told by Sin (i.e., The Devil) to "vamp" (i.e., seduce) the Tramp (Chaplin). The winged nymphet and the Tramp kissed before her Sweetheart arrived. She and her Sweetheart, who was played by a man who appeared to be a lot older than even 32-year-old Chaplin, kissed before he allowed the nymphet and the Tramp to embrace and kiss again. However, after the nymphet refused to release her embrace of the Tramp, her Sweetheart became jealous and pummeled the Tramp.

Lillita went on to become Chaplin's young wife and subsequently write a tell-all - *My Life With Chaplin: An Intimate Memoir*, which may give us some insight to what Franco was referencing about Chaplin's fun.

Lillita shared in the memoir that she first met Chaplin on April 15, 1914 - her sixth birthday. After Lita's mother spotted

Chaplin sitting in the rear of a restaurant, she asked the owner, "Do you think it would disturb Mr. Chaplin if my daughter were introduced to him?" The owner replied, "[...] I'm sure it'll be all right. He's very flattered when the children want to meet him, but he's shy of grownups" Upon meeting Lita, Chaplin opined, "Hasn't she lovely dark eyes and hair?"

By the time Lita was 12, the "incredibly shy" Chaplin had become one of the most famous men on the planet and arguably the most famous man in the United States, which is why when 29-year-old Chaplin married 16-year-old Mildred Harris he only: "[…] drew gasps and condemnations only from a small section of the public."

Lita met Chaplin again six years later after Chuck Riesner, Chaplin's assistant director, offered Lita a small but controversial part in the previously mentioned *The Kid*. When Lita visited Chaplin's studio to the sign the contract, she was offered the opportunity to meet Chaplin. In anticipation of meeting him, the previous day Lita stood: "[…] in front of her full-length mirror, melodramatically posing and admiring [her] developing breasts." Chaplin, in his mid-thirties, opined to 12-year-old Lita, "You're an extremely pretty child, my dear and I'm glad Mr. Riesner found you."

After Chaplin had a company artist paint a likeness of Lita similar to the girl in Sir Joshua Reynolds' 'Age of Innocence', Lita began to "catch" Chaplin looking at her with a "rapt expression". She wrote: "It was an expression I couldn't define, but it made me feel strange." After Chaplin showed Lita the painting, he confessed, "I've been peeking at you, my dear, when you haven't been looking.

I've been more and more drawn to those fascinating eyes of yours. They're so very young [...] And only twelve years old! Amazing!"

Using a seduction technique that Royal encouraged in *The Pimp Game*, one that Robert Beck shared in *Iceberg Slim, The Lost Interviews*, and one that the Milner's discovered in Black Players, *The Secret World of Black Pimps*, Lita wrote that Chaplin: "[...] had a reputation for hibernating after a picture [...]" and that after *The Kid* was completed she: "[...] saw Chaplin rarely or not at all." She wrote: "I discovered myself missing him, missing the fuss he made over me [...] I had developed a twelve-year-old's crush on him, and I could hardly wait to see him again."

On the first day back at the studio and after the New York premier of *The Kid*, Chaplin invited Lita, unchaperoned, to a birthday party for Mae Collins at his home; however, Lita's mother overheard the conversation, rejected the invitation and "steered" Lita home. Subsequently, Chaplin gave Lita and her mother the "cold shoulder" and at the end of the year, Lita's option on her contract was not picked up.

Lita wrote that as she was nearing her 15th birthday, sex was "uppermost" in her mind "a great portion of the time". Thus, Lita was enthralled by the stories that her good friend Merna Kennedy shared. Merna who was approximately five months younger than Lita had "brick-red hair, fair skin and blue eyes". Lita pleaded with Merna, "Gee, I'm hardly fifteen!" Merna replied, "If you're big enough, you're old enough." Merna shared with Lita that she had lost her virginity at the age of 13 and had subsequently had sex with "five boys and one man".

By the age of 15, Lita, although still a virgin, had become self-assured enough to pursue a role in Chaplin's *The Gold Rush*. After Lita got the part, she had "wishful daydreams" of Chaplin making love to her. She was certain that it would never happen since her mother was "zealously against" it. However, she was: "[...] consumed by the fantasy of being held and kissed and protected by Charlie."

Lita recalled the moment that it became "incontestably clear" that Charlie was sexually attracted to her as well. It was: "at lunch in the dining car on the way to Truckee [to shoot scenes for *The Gold Rush*]." She wrote: "Charlie was lunching with two studio workers at his table, and Mama and I were lunching at the table directly across the narrow aisle. He glanced up and saw me, and from the way he looked at me I suddenly got the feeling that he was seeing me for the first time – and that he very much approved of what he saw. All the guardedness, all his reserve was stripped away, and his distinctly intimate gaze sent erotic waves across the aisle that a shiver tore through me."

While in Truckee, Lita was told by Henry Bergman, "Charlie wonders why you haven't dropped by to say hello." 15-year-old Lita, with her mother bedridden with the flu, almost immediately sauntered to Chaplin's room. Here is a summary of what took place after some bantering:

Chaplin's hands circled Lita's waist and pulled the nymphet closer to him. Then he "roughly" pushed her onto the bed before he kissed her mouth and neck and caressed her body. Lita asked Chaplin, who was in a pair of red silk pajamas, to, "Please...stop...", but he covered her "mouth with a deep-drawn kiss" and clutched her breast "with almost brutal force." Lita pleaded with Chaplin to stop, which he did, but forewarned, "I'm going to make love to you. When the time and the place is right, we're going to make love."

Despite Chaplin's aggression and Lita's (dis)pleasure with Chaplin's hour of "erotic scrutiny", Lita decided that if she and Chaplin were alone again, she would be: "[…] ready for him. Eagerly ready."

After they arrived back in Los Angeles, Chaplin convinced Lita's mother to allow Lita to be seen with him in public as his protégée for publicity purposes. He assured her that they would not be attending "premieres and dinner parties alone" but that his fiancée, Thelma Morgan Converse, would be the third wheel. Lita's mother agreed, but even Lita knew that her mother "was making a big mistake".

Consequently, Chaplin was able to get Lita alone at the relaxing Santa Monica Swimming Club. Chaplin brushed Lita's ear and neck with his lips before he lowered Lita's bathing suit straps and palmed her "tingling breasts in his palms." Lita "aggressively" threw her arms around Chaplin and hugged him - "bringing him closer". Chaplin then "peeled" the bathing suit completely off of Lita and muttered to himself, "Beautiful, incredibly beautiful..." However, after Chaplin lowered himself and began "moving with small, steady increases of force", Lita pleaded, "No. Oh, I can't, I can't!" But after Chaplin informed Lita that the pain would have quickly ceased after her hymen broke, Lita asked, "Why-didn't you keep on, then?" Charlie sympathetically replied, "Because you were so fearful."

After dinner at Musso Frank's Restaurant, in the back seat of Chaplin's large limousine, Chaplin's "soft hand dug into the bodice" of Lita's dress, "[h]is other hand darted under" Lita's skirt and "danced" up her thigh until it found her "underpants". Chaplin "found his way to the top of the elastic banded underpants, and wordlessly he yanked them down"; however, the pain was still too intense for Lita. Thus, once again Chaplin mercifully stopped.

But three days later, Charlie announced that he had a "blistering headache", dismissed everyone from the set except Lita, and proceeded to take her virginity in the steam room of Chaplin's Cove Way mansion. Lita wrote: "The pain blinded me far more than the encircling steam, but I writhed wildly, as though in ecstasy [...] I was fifteen, but I felt younger than fifteen."

In addition, Lita noted Chaplin's nympholepsy. She imparted: "It's hardly a secret that Charlie had a penchant for young girls. He approached them as projects, and indeed, cared for them. He liked to cultivate them, to gain their trust, to be their first - never their second or third lover, and to create them as scrupulously as he created a motion picture. To me he admitted his preference for the company of inexperienced girls over experienced women. '[...] The most beautiful form of human life is the very young girl just starting to bloom [...]'"

Now, let's take a look at Woody Allen and see what fun he has had as an actor, director and writer. And let's begin by perusing his filmography that includes at least nine films that Allen has written and/or directed that contains at least one age-discrepant relationships:

Play It Again, Sam (1972): A female character shared with Allan (Woody Allen), "Allen, I won't deny it. I'm a nymphomaniac. I discovered sex very early. I slept with everybody. My schoolteacher."

Love and Death (1975): Ninety-year-old Father Andre, the "Holiest of Holies, Ancient and Wise" advised, "I have lived many years. And after many trials and tribulations. I have come to [the] conclusion that the best thing is blonde twelve-year-old girls. Two of them, whenever possible."

Manhattan (1979): Forty-two-year-old Isaac (Woody Allen), a comedy writer and aspiring novelist, ended his affair with a 17-year-old high school student (Mariel Hemingway) to be with an older woman (Diane Keaton) - only to regret it later.

Katie Duggan wrote in the article "The Women of the Woody Allen Papers", which was published in *The Nassau Weekly* that a draft of *Manhattan's* script, which is archived in one of 56 boxes in the rare-books wing of Princeton's Firestone Library, revealed that Hemingway's character was originally sixteen - an "infant". And Stacey Nelkin related on *The Howard Stern Show* that *Manhattan* was based on her relationship with Allen that began after they met on the set of *Annie Hall*. Nelkin was a 17-year-old student at Manhattan's prestigious Stuyvesant high school, and Allen was 42.

Allen confirmed the relationship in "Woody Allen Speaks Out" a 2014 Op-Ed piece in the *New York Times.*

Babi Christina Engelhardt opined in Gary Baum's *Hollywood Reporter* piece "Woody Allen's Secret Teen Lover Speaks: Sex, Power and a Conflicted Muse Who Inspired 'Manhattan'" that Stacey Nelkin was <u>not</u> the sole inspiration for *Manhattan* (1979). Babi presumed that she, Nelkin *and* the two "beautiful young [lipstick lesbian] ladies" were the inspiration for the critically acclaimed and award-winning film. Let's learn more about Engelhardt and see what would give her that impression.

In the "Allen, Woody: Director" section of the *New York Magazine* cover story "Who Was Jeffrey Epstein Calling? A Close study of his circle - social, professional, transactional - reveals a damning portrait of elite New York" it states:

> For years before his relationship with Mia Farrow, Allen had carried on with a 16-year-old girl he'd met at Elaine's named Babi Christina Engelhardt [...] Engelhardt had sex with Allen more than 100 times, she says, sometimes with [Mia] Farrow [or with two other "beautiful young ladies" in his Central Park facing 930 Fifth Ave bedroom]." (In addition, Engelhardt related that she had had [lipstick] lesbian sex *before* she met Woody.)

Engelhardt provided the details of her relationship with Woody with Baum. Baum wrote that, which is absolutely no surprise to me, that the "confident" Engelhardt "brazenly" initiated the affair with Woody:

Sixteen, emerald-eyed, blond, an aspiring model with a confident streak and a painful past: Babi Christina Engelhardt had just caught Woody Allen's gaze at legendary New York City power restaurant Elaine's. It was October 1976, and when Engelhardt returned from the ladies' room, she dropped a note on his table with her phone number. It brazenly read: "Since you've signed enough autographs, here's mine!"

Soon, Allen rang, inviting her to his Fifth Avenue penthouse. The already-famous 41-year-old director [...] never asked her age. But she told him she was still in high school [...]. Within weeks, they'd become physically intimate at his place. She wouldn't turn 17, legal in New York, until that December.

The pair embarked on, by her account, a clandestine romance of eight years [...]

Engelhardt confessed that she "liked" Woody and finds him "so interesting" because "his wit is magnetic" and that "[...] he was charming and alluring."
Baum wrote of Engelhardt:

She's proud of her teenage self as an up-by-her-bootstraps heroine who successfully beguiled a "celebrated genius." Even now, she holds herself largely responsible for remaining in the relationship as long as she did [...]. She considered him then, and still considers him now, a Great Man.

Husbands and Wives (1992): Gabe Roth (Woody Allen), a literature professor, began a relationship with one of his students (Juliette Lewis) after she read and praised the manuscript of his new novel. However, prior to taking Roth's class, Rain had previous relationships with three (much) older men: her father's close friend, her father's business partner, and her analyst.

Deconstructing Harry (1997): writer Harry Block (Woody Allen) drove a prostitute, a friend, and his kidnapped son, to his former university to receive an honorary degree. One of the sub-plots involved Harry's relationship with Fay (Elisabeth Shue), a young fan who turned into a follower, then a pupil - Eliza Doolittle style, and finally into a roommate. Despite warning Fay to avoid falling in love with him and confessing his intention to "fuck" her before moving on to the next fan, Harry fell in love with Fay and was distraught to learn that she got engaged to Larry (Billy Crystal) - Harry's "alleged" friend.

Whatever Works (2009): Boris Yellnikoff (Larry David), a middle-aged quantum mechanics professor at Columbia University, reluctantly married Melodie Saint Ann Celestine (Evan Rachel Wood), a young runaway from Mississippi.

You Will Meet a Tall Dark Stranger (2010): Alfie (Anthony Hopkins), an elderly man, left his wife to marry a young call girl, while Roy (Josh Brolin), a middle-aged novelist, became engrossed by Dia

(Freida Pinto), a beautiful young woman, while desperately trying to get his second book published.

Irrational Man (2015): Abe Lucas (Joaquin Phoenix), a philosophy professor at Braylin, found himself in a life crisis, but he gained a new purpose in life after he began a relationship with Jill Pollard (Emma Stone), one of his students, and became a one-man vigilante.

A Rainy Day in New York (2019): Ashleigh (Elle Fanning), a Yardley college student, was involved in not one, not two, not three but (possibly) four age-gap affairs. In the film, after Gatsby (Timothée Chalamet) and Ashleigh (Elle Fanning), both Yardley students, visited New York City, Ashleigh became infatuated with Roland Pollard (51-year-old Liev Schreiber), a famous film director, whom she desired to interview for the school's paper. Ashleigh said referring to Roland, "I can see why all the leading ladies fall in love with him."

Later in the film, Roland asked, "I want us to get to know each other Ashleigh. Would you consider coming with me to the South of France?" That left Gatsby wondering, "What the hell is it about older guys that seem so appealing to women [...] All they are is [*sic*] decrepit. What's sexy about short term memory loss [...]"

Moments later, Gatsby ran into Chan (Selena Gomez), a fashion student at New York's Fashion Institute of Technology, whom had a date with a, "[...] very handsome, very rich [and] very clever" dermatologist. In addition, Chan was the younger sister of Amy - Gatsby's gorgeous and sexually advanced Jewish high school sweetheart.

Gatsby said, "Amy was gorgeous and so sexually advanced. Word on Amy was she performed oral sex at a Bar Mitzvah. I think they should make that a part of every Jewish holiday [...] And what a great Hanukkah gift."

While accompanied by Ashleigh, Ted Davidoff (46-year-old Jude Law), a writer, gets into an argument with his wife whom assumes that Ashleigh is Ted's 15-year-old concubine. Subsequently, Ashleigh met the actor Francisco Vega (39-year-old Diego Luna). Francisco asked. "Do you have a boyfriend?" To which Ashleigh replied, "He's a mere youth." Consequently, after a joint and some whiskey, the age-gap couple proceeded to have sex until Francisco's girlfriend arrived unexpectedly.

In the end, Gatsby summed up *A Rainy Day in New York* well when he said to Ashleigh, "You were loved spiritually, emotionally, and physically by three different gifted men."

Duggan related that Allen wrote in his notes that Ashleigh: "[…] should not be 20 or 21. Sounds more like 18—or even 17—but 18 seems better."

Rifkin's Festival (2020): While attending the San Sebastián International Film, Mort Rifkin (76-year-old Wallace Shawn) fell in love with Jo Rojas (44-year-old Elena Anaya), but more relevantly, Rojas had a previous affair with her college professor before he left her for another student. (Chaplin was named dropped as well as Éric Rohmer's *Claire's Knee* (1970), which is essentially about a nympholept-nymphet-nymphet love triangle.)

So, what did Franco mean when he wrote that it's usually no fun to be the actor, director and writer of a film unless you're Charlie Chaplin or Woody Allen? Could one justifiably infer that Franco was referring to Chaplin's and Allen's (on and off the screen) nympholepsy? Probably.

Now back to *Actors Anonymous: A Novel* where Franco often wrote about the perils of fame. For example: "[…] I'm like Santa Claus: Everyone needs a picture siting on my knee. The ones I don't mind are the young pretty ones."

The protagonist had sex with a drunk and unconscious girl in her Ohio University dorm room, but despite the fact that she was a college coed, she was described as: "[…] a little blond girl, pretty cute." Freshman?

The famous ephebophile Charlie Chaplin was mentioned *again*: "My stare was the stare of an uncompromising carnivore that saw her young flesh as food; like Chaplin's companion in *The Gold Rush* who is transformed […] into the Platonic form of the Female, a pinup bent-over in a tingly blue G-string. She was only eleven, but I never broke my vampiric stare as I went through our moves with the other zombies."

It's imparted in the novel that: "Errol Flynn once owned a Gaugin painting, but he had to sell it when he became dissolute and was two million in debt […]" As it relates, Beverly Aadland's mother wrote in her book *The Beautiful Pervert*: "My Beverly was only fifteen and still a virgin when she met [48-year-old] Errol Flynn. A few hours later, she was still fifteen…but she wasn't a virgin anymore." Beverly went on to co-star with Flynn in *Cuban Rebel Girls* (1959). And Darwin Porter and Danforth Prince alleged in

Elizabeth Taylor: There is Nothing Like a Dame that 15-year-old Taylor was bedded by Flynn after he got her tipsy on pink champagne.

As it relates to Gaugin, Nancy Mathews related in *Paul Gauguin: An Erotic Life* that thirteen-year-old Teha'amana was offered to Gauguin by her mother and that: "[...] Western tourists were commonly offered young girls, usually by the girl's parents, to serve as companions [...]" and that Gauguin had a "[...] genuine delight at having an adolescent lover [...]".

Back again to *Actors Anonymous: A Novel*, where The Actor had a beautiful girlfriend, but that didn't prevent him from having: "[…] an uncontrollable need to fuck every young thing he could. In France that summer, he "fucked" at least one "young thing" and elaborated: "[…] there was something nice about fooling around with her young body and having her say things like "You're fucking the mayor's daughter" over and over […]" And the Villain disclosed: "[…] I was in Paris sleeping with college girls literally half my age, but underneath I have a good heart. Just as The Actor had a good heart."

Kim was carried out by two orderlies, "grunting and thrashing", but, inadvertently, her "flat young chest was exposed for all to see." 17-year-old Cent, the star of "*Day's End*, a film about teenage vampires […] was screwing the thirty-eight-year-old producer, Mark Steely." And lastly, The Actor had "a lifelong love of literature" that wasn't shared by his father who didn't care about The Actor's: "[…] discovery of Dostoevsky's *Underground Man*, or Raskolnikov, or Hamsun's *Hunger.*" *Underground Man* is the protagonist in Dostoevsky's *Notes from Underground.* In part two of the novella, 40-year-old Underground Man had a brief sexual affair with Liza, a young prostitute whom had been sold into prostitution by her family. [Oh, and this reminds me that Woody Allen appears to be a huge fan of Dostoevsky as Allen mentioned the famous Russian novelist in a number of movies like *Husbands and Wives* (1992) and *Rifkins Festival* (2020).]

Per Amazon, in *Hollywood Dreaming: Stories, Pictures and Poems*: "[...] James Franco reflects on his life in Hollywood and beyond through an intimate and powerful series of poems, artwork, and short stories."

In "Becoming An Introduction", in reference to Shakespeare's *King Lear*, Franco composed: "I don't want to be Lear, I want to be Lear's Fool. Lear has to worry about politics; the Fool gets to say whatever he wants." Then Franco explained *his* Lear: "*My* Lear is God, [and] young women from age fifteen to twenty-nine [...]" Franco did not elaborate on why <u>his</u> *Lear* includes nymphets, but if we stay with our theme of nympholepsy, it's worth mentioning that while the age of consent, thanks to lobbying feminists, is 16 in most of the United States (e.g., New Jersey), Franco, who has read extensively, may be referring to across the pond where in Japan it's 13, in Germany it's 14, and in France the age of consent is a, comparatively, whopping 15. However, Franco did share: "This is not a book. It is a sculpture that you open, like my body and mind were opened [...]" And while it's confirmed that Juliet of Shakespeare's *Romeo and Juliet* was 13 at the beginning of the love story, King Lear described Cordelia as "So young and so cruel?", "worthless little thing", and "a girl I hate." In addition, unlike her sisters, Cordelia wasn't married. Lear: "The two great princes of France and Burgundy, vying for the hand of my youngest Cordelia."

The chapter "Sprang Brake" is inspired by the film *Spring Breakers* (2012). Here's IMDb's plot summary:

Four college girls hold up a restaurant in order to fund their spring break vacation. While partying, drinking, and taking drugs, they are arrested, only to be bailed out by [Alien (James Franco)] a drug and arms dealer.

When *Spring Breakers* was filmed, 19-year-old Selena Gomez was the youngest of her female castmates, but the fact that approximately 23-year-old Vanessa Hudgens was a former Disney star and there were nude selfies of her on the Internet made her role more tantalizing. And the fact that, approximately, 22-year-old Ashley Benson played a high school student on the popular but controversial teen drama *Pretty Little Liars* was intriguing as well. During that same year, one could watch Benson play a high school student on television and watch her in a threesome with Franco and a former Disney girl in the theater. (Interestingly, Franco named dropped Benson and *Pretty Little Liars* in the previously mentioned *New York Times* piece on "The Meanings of the Selfie".)

Franco wrote about the threesome, which included lipstick lesbianism, in the poem "Florida Sex Scene" published in *Strongest of the Litter*:

One more layer of deadly bubble
Gum. When we did the ménage
À trois in the pool at midnight
The girls were drunk.

It was the sweetest thing.

The had taken shots in their trailer

Because it was their first sex scene.

In the pool we went at it.

And between takes, while they reset the lights

The beautiful blond one-

A realization of someone's dream-

Stayed in my arms and told me

Everything she loved about my work.

Let's review. The beautiful blond one, the realization of someone's dream, stayed in Franco's arms and told him everything she loved about his work. But Franco didn't share whom was dreaming of beautiful blond Benson.

In addition, to a number of alluring photos of the young bikini clad *Spring Breakers*, which included some belfies, *Hollywood Dreaming* contains three poems that Franco was aroused to compose: "Young Bitches", "Like a Mug Shot", and "Angelz".

In "Young Bitches", Franco referred to his young co-stars as "bitches, young and curvy". And he mentioned that being young is what made his co-stars "the objects of the ruling class". Franco composed that Harmony [Korine], the film's writer and director, "plucked" the actresses from *Teen Vogue* and: "paraded [them] around like baubles (i.e., "a showy, usually cheap, ornament" [Dictionary.com]). But Franco wrote that:

[...] what they didn't know was that their value

Was their gingerbread forms, their sweet sugar bodies,

And these were the things that Director puppeted about.

Sweet. Sugar. Bodies. Charles Bukowski and Frederick Seidel would be proud. And I couldn't help but wonder if Selena Gomez, Vanessa Hudgens, Ashley Benson and Rachel Korine were aware of the fact that, as Franco shared, Harmony Korine, puppeted their sweet sugar bodies to sell movie tickets. For example, in the film, while the professor lectured, Korine had Benson's character share, "I love penis" before Hudgens' character simulated oral sex. Later, after the college coeds robbed a diner, Hudgens said, "Seeing all this money makes my pussy wet." Instead of going to a private bathroom stall, Korine had the girls move their bikini bottoms to the side and pee - in public. And it appears from the film that Korine is <u>not</u> a boob-man but an (young) ass-man. However, Josh Eells, opined in his *Rolling Stone* piece, "Inside 'Spring Breakers,' the Most Debauched Movie of the Year", that Korine portrayed a: "[…] kind of girl-power camaraderie that could almost be called feminist." Lastly, although, as I mentioned, Selena Gomez was 19 when *Spring Breakers* was filmed, she appeared to be a younger nymphet. Consequently, Franco's character asked Faith - Gomez's character:

"What's your name?"

"Faith"

"Faith? That's a pretty name [...] I'm the answer to your prayers [...] How old are you? You look about 15. But

Later, before Faith tearily departed from the spring break festivities, Franco's character said: "God damn, I like you so much [...] I want you to know that I like you so much. I really do [...] And I wanna be thinking about you when I'm with your friends."

Wait, so does that mean that Franco's character was thinking of Faith, who appeared to be 15-years-old, when he was having a three-way with her schoolmates? Probably.

In "Like a Mug Shot", Franco referred to his young co-stars as "thangs" and implied that they were gifts: "Thangs all wrapped up in them bikinis like bows". But gifts to whom? Franco went on: "With dem ho, ho, hoes." And he wrote that the girls had "mug shot Faces too" due to coming from a world where: "Decency is doin' what Mommy says, except they got\Them [young] bodies that done got them all in twouble."

Also, Franco referred to his young co-stars as "Angelz". In this poem, he wrote that shooting the film, which was set and filmed in F-L-A (i.e., Florida): [...] was special, like a bubble, in which\We all lived, a magic time [...]" In the next stanza, he reiterated that the film: "[...] was special, because them girlz\Was doin' sumptin like this fo' the first time"

Franco went on to share that the girls were initially excited and "said yes, yes" but became "scared, and pulled back", when they didn't want to alienate: "[...] all them fanz\Of theirs, the young wunz, impressionable." However, when Franco arrived, everything changed, because he: "[...] waz the electricity that shocked dem\Into place [...]\They was hot young things with skillz of sex".

Franco ended "Angelz" by sharing that his presence alone "galvanized" the hot young things' sex skills and brought their sex skills "to the fore". ("Angelz" was accompanied by two belfies with Vanessa Hudgens in a [cheeky] thong.)

Before moving on, it's worth (briefly) going down another nympholepsy rabbit hole to discuss Benson's *Pretty Little Liars*. The ABC Family show was adapted from the series of Young\New Adult novels. Let's take a look at the first volume that was written by the national bestselling author Sara Shepard.

In the beginning of chapter three, Hanna, who Sara Shepard described as the most sought-after girl at Rosewood Day high school and her best friend, Mona Vanderwaal, were sipping red wine at the French-inspired cafe, Rive Gauch, in the King James Mall. While they were inconceivably enjoying their drinks and "comparing *Vogue* to *Teen Vogue*," Hanna noticed a "fortysomething guy staring lecherously at them". Logically, Mona decided it would be a good idea to have a "Lolita" moment.

"We should flash him." Mona suggested before the teens slowly pulled up the hems of their sky-high minis and revealed their panties to the, "regular Humbert Humbert."

"You know that guy had a boner," Mona presumed as the middle-aged man dashed away after spilling his drink.

Sara Shepard's website says that *Pretty Little Liars* "[…] is loosely based on Sara's experiences growing up on Philadelphia's Main Line." The nymphet's Philadelphia's Main Line sounds a lot like the ripened teens of Palo Alto.

On the *Pretty Little Liars* television show, Aria, a 16-year-old brunette, met Eric at a bar, kissed him and "made out" with him in the bar's bathroom. The next day she found out that Eric was actually Mr. Fitz, her new English teacher. Aria and Mr. Fitz continued to make out in subsequent episodes in his car and his apartment. However, Mr. Fitz repeatedly tried to end the age-gap affair, not because he felt that the relationship was inappropriate due to their age difference, but out of fear of losing his (high school) teaching position. Only the naïve would be surprised that 16-year-old Aria was the aggressor in the age-gap affair and that *she* desperately wanted the relationship with her English teacher to continue.

The "A Place in the Sun" section of *Hollywood Dreaming* takes us down another rabbit hole. First off, "A Place in the Sun I" mentions: "An indelible image that was Kerouac". We already mentioned Kerouac's classic *On The Road* and Dean's liaison in the Ace Hotel with 15-year-old Marylou - twice. It may be obvious to some that this section of the book is based on *A Place in the Sun* (1951), which is based on the novel and play *An American Tragedy* that is based on the murder of 20-year-old Grace Mae Brown by the hands of 23-year-old Chester Gillette – seemingly because Gillette didn't want Brown to give birth to their child. However, the film made several intriguing modifications to the official non-fiction story. For instance, Shelley Winters played a character based on Grace Mae Brown, but Winters was approximately 31-years-old when the film was filmed. Montgomery Clift played a character based on Chester Gillette but Clift was approximately 31-years-old when the film was filmed. But Clift's character not only killed Winters' character because she was pregnant but because Clift was in love with Angela Vickers - a "society girl", whom was played by a stunning approximately 18-year-old Elizabeth Taylor. Franco wrote two versions of the poem "Montgomery Clift". One in *Hollywood Dreaming* and another in *Strongest of the Litter*.

Franco didn't reveal her age, but he shared in "A Place in the Sun I" that he watched *A Place in the Sun* (1951) with a:

> [...] part-Irish, Part-Cherokee beauty, with a cheekbone
> face
> And a long elfin body to match, slung
> In a cherry-red G-string and nothing else, bundled
> In a cloud of Chateau sheets [...]

And Franco's half-nude beauty commented on the "[...] beauty of young society Liz;"

Franco opined in "A Place in the Sun II", that Clift's performance in *A Place in the Sun* (1951) was "defined and remarkable". And in "A Place in the Sun III", Franco described Liz as: "A young woman\angel, the actual Vickers,\An apparition too good to be fucked-" Franco even wrote that he couldn't "blame" Clift's character whom he described as: "[...] the hero for sinking ship,\And jumping ship, when one ship was loaded\With a *baby on board*; and the Shelly Winters" As for Liz, Franco wrote: "One, mamma mia, what a performance [...] I'm in love." But as for the older Winters, he wrote: "Goes to show you, there is no hope\For the ugly. All we want is Monty and Liz\To love and love and love [...]"

You may ask, "What's Franco's favorite film?" He imparted in "A Place in the Sun V" that it's, you guessed it, *A Place in the Sun* (1951). Why? It's because of the:

> [...] angelic filter shots
> Of Angela Vickers - that's Elizabeth Taylor -
> Beauty shots that establish her as the young man's
> Objex of desire, establish his subjective lust.

In "A Place in the Sun VI", Franco touched upon an interesting yet widely misunderstood phenomenon. "He [Clift's character] convinced himself that he could love Shelly Winters before he knew\He could have Elizabeth Taylor. I know I've done the same," And Franco is not alone, and I would surmise that that is what happened to most active nympholepts. I say, the difference between an active nympholept and an inactive nympholept is an active nymphet. For example, in teacher-student affairs, the common perception is that the teachers initiated the relationships, but just like in *Pretty Little Liars* and in almost every piece of fiction - whether it be watched in the theater, streamed on Netflix or a read in a novel or novella, nymphets are almost always the initiators of the age-gap affairs. This even includes Nabokov's *Lolita* of which the novelist Robertson Davies' opined that *Lolita* was: "[...] not the corruption of an innocent child by a cunning adult, but the exploitation of a weak adult by a corrupt child." Furthermore, most men don't have the self-confidence to imagine that they would be attractive to a nymphet - let alone possess the charisma and skills to seduce a nubile teen. However, once a coed has expressed her attraction to a teacher or, *àla American Beauty* (1999), a nymphet expresses her attraction to her best friend's dad, then dormant nympholepsy is awakened, which, per Ridley's *The Red Queen,* is something that is inherent in all (heteronormative) men. And as the saying goes, art [very often] imitates life. Remember when 16-year-old Engelhardt dropped her phone number on Woody Allen's table?

Before continuing with *Hollywood Dreaming,* let's go back to *Palo Alto* and back to *Fast Times at Ridgemont High,* which is based on Cameron Crowe's nonfiction book *Ridgemont High: A True Story* that elaborates on Stacy's age-gap relationship with Ron Johnson. In the non-fiction book, 15-year-old Stacy was distraught because, despite having been on two dates with 25-year-old Johnson, he hadn't made an effort to take her virginity. 17-year-old Linda, who had just finished her sophomore year at Ridgemont high, said in reaction to Stacy's dismay:

> "I don't believe this guy," said Linda. "You know what he reminds me of? The words fell from her lips like spoiled clams: "*A high school boy.* Haven't you figured men out yet, Stacy? Most guys are just … pussies. For years I chased after every guy I thought was cute. I thought if I was nice to them, they'd get the idea and call me up. Well, guess what? They didn't call. I got impatient. So, *I* started making the first move, and you know what else? Most guys are just too insecure and too chicken to do it for themselves."
>
> "I don't care *who* he is," Linda continued. "Two dates is *enough*. Are you sure he's not a fag?"

The *naiveté* surrounding the sexual nature of nymphets is what led to the age of consent laws. Per Odem, until 1897, the age of consent in California and in most United States was 10. It was 12 in seven states. And it was 7 in Delaware! How did the ages get so low? Our early age of consent laws originated over the pond. And how did the age go from ten to seventeen (in most states)? One word - feminists.

Odem wrote that after the 19th century, a number of young women started working outside of the home and consequently became more promiscuous. Feminists blamed the raunchy behavior on "dirty old men" who paid for the services of nymphet prostitutes. Consequently, the feminists successfully lobbied to have the age of consent raised; however, it backfired, because a number of young women became even more licentious.

As a result, feminists realized that issues like abuse, education, and poverty had more to do with the nymphet's erratic behavior than "dirty old men", but it was too late. The damage had already been done - the age of consent laws had been changed. However, there were two unsuccessful attempts to lower the age of consent. In 1889, there was an effort in Kansas to lower the age to twelve, and in 1890, there was an attempt in New York to lower the age to fourteen.

Back to "A Place in the Sun VI" where Franco wrote the line: "Except I don't try for the Liz Taylors anymore; if they come, they come [...] And most times they'll be nice ones - especially if you're a movie star." And speaking of movie stars and age-gap affairs, Franco wrote in parenthesis: "(I like how Liz comforted Monty in the film and like she did in life.)"

Unsurprisingly, per Petersen's *Scandals of Classic Hollywood: Sex, Deviance, and Drama from the Golden Age of American Cinema,* Charlie Chaplin opined that *A Place in the Sun* (1951) was "the greatest movie made about America".

Part II of *Hollywood Dreaming* includes the poem "Sean II" that is partially based on Sean Penn's role in *Fast Times at Ridgemont High* (1982). And I learned from "Rolm/Zoo", a "shrimp" story, that 23-year-old Ollie Bacon had: "[...] gotten a teenage girl pregnant." "It sounds like the girl's parents are pressing charges," said Mrs. Hello.

Franco embedded a short story inside the short story "Grand Illusion". #meta. In the short story within the short story, some American soldiers were bathing in a French river. "Then three French girls came over to the side of the river. They were giggling and talking in French." Subsequently: "At lights out, the soldiers pretended to go to sleep, and then they snuck out at midnight. They went over to the French girls' house [...]" At the French girls' house: "Duke [an American soldier] and Bianca [a French girl] went into the only bedroom. All three girls normally slept in the same bed [...]" Then: "Marianna [a French girl] led Tim [an American soldier] out to a barn that was near the house [...] They went into one of the stables and lay down in the straw. They kissed and made love." After suffering a devastating injury in Germany, Tim returned to France to rekindle his romance with the French girl.

Franco didn't give the ages of the French girls, but his use of "giggling", "girls" and the fact that they "normally slept in the same bed" *may* be telling. And this sentence *may* be telling: "The only problem was that there were only three *girls* and there were four *guys*." [Emphasis mine] Why not three girls and three boys? Who knows? Franco.

In "Grand Illusion", Shrimp, the author of the short story about the French girls, was taken to Kepler's Books by his grandparents. "Shrimp found a book by the actor Barry Dennen; it was called *My Life with Barbara: A Love Story*. In the book, Barry said that he took Barbra Streisand's virginity [only days after she became of California legal age. Per Mann's *Hello Gorgeous: Becoming Barbra Streisand*: "she had just turned eighteen".

"Bungalow 89" in Part III The Actor Stories has a number of nympholepsy rabbit holes that I won't enter but let's take a peek inside. Franco mentioned Leonardo DiCaprio's role in Woody Allen's *Celebrity* (1998), but I won't fully discuss, until later, 22-year-old Camila Morrone's Instagram story where she responded to trolls who questioned her two-year age-gap affair with 44-year-old DiCaprio. I'm surprised the trolling didn't commence when Morrone was 19 and DiCaprio was 42. We already discussed Woody Allen. I won't fully discuss Terry Richardson who shot the behind the scenes photos of Franco's Oscars hosting gig. Richardson's rabbit hole would go from his *Glee GQ* photoshoot of which The Parents Television Council released a report saying that Richardson's photographs sexualized actresses who play high school-aged students, bordered on pedophilia and were nearly pornographic. And I won't discuss Lea Michele, *Glee's* star, who was 14-years-old when she began playing Wendla Bergman in the controversial teen play *Spring Awakening*, which included teen masturbation, teen BDSM, teen sex and father-daughter incest.

However, with a title like "Vice", how can I not go down a hole and find a nympholept and a nymphet? Franco related that he wrote a "a little thing" for *Vice* which was "J. D. Salinger's War: The book about Salinger is better than the movie". Franco's *Vice* piece was based on Salerno and Shields' *Salinger* where they wrote about Salinger: "[...] trying to catch the young *wuns* before they went over the cliff [...]".

Also, Salerno directed *Salinger* (2013). Scherstuhl's *Village Voice* review of the documentary "Salinger Would Make Holden Caulfield Puke" elaborated on Salinger's nympholepsy. The review mentioned that Salinger was "enraged that Charlie Chaplin, well past 50, once stole his girlfriend." The article was referring to Oona O'Neill, the daughter of playwright Eugene O'Neill. Salinger's affair started when O'Neill was 16 and he was approximately 22 but ended after the Pearl Harbor attack sent Salinger to the Army. Consequently, O'Neill moved from New York to Los Angeles and married 55-year-old Chaplin - very soon after she turned 18.

But before Oona married Chaplin, she dated Peter Arno – a cartoonist and (open) nympholept. Per Ben Schwartz's *Vanity Fair* cover story "The Double Life of Peter Arno, *The New Yorker'*s Most Influential Cartoonist": "In 1942, [38-year-old Peter] Arno dated his last "Debutante of the Year," Oona O'Neill, 17-year-old daughter of Eugene O'Neill and future wife of Charlie Chaplin. Jane Scovell, Oona's biographer, shared: "Oona only slept with two men before she married Chaplin. Peter Arno and Orson

Welles. She was looking for older men, some sort of validation from them." Wait, Orson Welles too? But why did it have to be that Oona was seeking validation? Maybe, like a number of teens, she was simply attracted to older men. (Per Schwartz, prior to Oona, 34-year-old Arno dated 17-year-old Brenda Diana Duff Frazier - the original celebutante.)

In addition, Salerno related in his documentary that when Salinger was 30, he told 14-year-old Jean Miller, "I'd like to kiss you goodbye, but you know I can't." And he told Miller's mother, "I'm going to marry your daughter." Salinger and Miller reunited in Manhattan after Miller turned eighteen. Their relationship was platonic until *Miller* took the initiative to make it sexual. Sadly, the age-gap couple never married.

According to Alexander's *New York* magazine piece "J. D. Salinger's Women", after Salinger finished his stint in the military and moved to Cornish, New Hampshire, he [boldly] started entertaining high school girls and openly "escorted teenage girls to school dances and sporting events." Those exploits lead Salinger to meet 19-year-old Radcliffe preppy Claire Douglas. Salinger and Douglas eventually married and had two children. The marriage lasted a little over a decade until Douglas filed for divorce after Salinger continued to lock himself in his writing studio for over fourteen days at a time. #writerslife

Subsequently, Salinger was so impressed by Joyce Maynard's *New York Times'* cover story "An Eighteen Year Old Looks Back On Life" that he snail-mailed her via the *New York Times.* After they wrote each other approximately twenty-five letters, Maynard visited Salinger in New Hampshire, withdrew from

Yale, and moved in with the author. The affair ended abruptly after ten months.

Joyce Maynard summarized her affair with J.D. Salinger in the preface of the 2013 edition of *At Home in the World: A Memoir*. She shared:

> "I did not seek out J.D. Salinger. He wrote me a letter. I was eighteen years old. He was fifty-three."
>
> "By July, I'd moved in with him, and in September I gave up my little off-campus apartment and my scholarship and withdrew from Yale."
>
> "But I had loved him once, and more even than loved, had worshipped him."
>
> "He told me what movies to watch, what music to listen to, what food to eat. Jerry told me what to think, and write, and not write, what was real and what was false. He told me who to be, and because I adored him, I wanted to be that person."
>
> "The relationship lasted just eleven months, and ended [...] when I was nineteen years old."

In chapter five, Joyce wrote that Salinger followed up his letters by inviting her to "spend the weekend." And that her mother was "very proud" that Joyce had: "[...] attracted the attention of such a famous and brilliant man." During Joyce's first visit, Jerry did not attempt to have sex with her, but they kissed.

Until her next visit, Joyce and Salinger spoke on the phone "[...] every night, and sometimes in the day [...]" The letters continued too.

Ten days after Joyce started working at *The New York Times*, Jerry drove five hours to pick her up. They purchased: "[...] a bag of bagels and lox on the Upper West Side". Then Jerry drove: "[....] very fast, the full five hours straight back to New Hampshire." Joyce wrote: "This time, when I walk into his house, I know where I'm headed (i.e., to Jerry's bedroom where Joyce stood at the foot of his bed in one of her "short little-girl dresses")."

It turns out that that was the beginning of the end of their age-gap affair, because Salinger opined that Joyce was "shallow", "worthless", "corrupted", "worldly", "greedy", and "hungry" for (writing) fame. In addition, despite a number of failed treatments, Joyce suffered from severe "tightness of the muscles surrounding the vagina" and, consequently, could only perform oral sex on Salinger.

Joyce wrote that after they left a doctor's office for the last time: "Jerry Salinger put those fifty-dollar bills in my hand and told me to clear my things out of his house [...]"

I already wrote that Porter and Prince wrote in *Elizabeth Taylor: There is Nothing Like a Dame* that J.D. Salinger opined after he met 15-year-old Taylor, "She is the most beautiful creature I have ever seen in my life." But Franco wrote of Salinger in his *Vice* piece that Salinger's relationship with Oona: "[...] showed him trying to capture Oona's type and age right before he lost her. He was trying to capture the lost innocence of his moment with her."

Franco is simply wrong here. I would argue that Salinger was not "trying to capture the lost innocence", but, like most men, Salinger was a nympholept, but unlike most men, Salinger simply had the self-confidence, that often comes with being an artist slash writer, to pursue nymphets.

And of Salinger's nympholepsy, Franco wrote in his *Vice* piece: "The whole thing is pretty icky [...] But it's not a surprise that the man who was obsessed with youth in his work would be obsessed with youth in his life." "Icky"? Really Franco? Did Franco just throw Salinger under an MTA bus? We're not halfway done with this book and one could argue strongly that *Franco* is the one who is "obsessed with youth in his work".

The next section of the "Vice" chapter contains a short story, which is based on the previous "Bungalow 89" chapter and a Franco *Vice* post "Bungalow 89 - A Short Story by James Franco". In this short story Franco analyzes "For Esmé—with Love and Squalor" from Salinger's *Nine Stories*:

> [...] "For Esmé," [...] a man goes to war, is traumatized, and then saved (or almost saved, but not quite, in "Dickfish") by the innocence of a young girl [...] And what do we say about this obsession with innocence?"

Instead of answering Franco's question about Salinger's "obsession with innocence", I'm going to respond by sharing that, per Wikipedia, "The pot calling the kettle black' is a proverbial idiom that may be of Spanish origin, of which English versions began to appear in the first half of the 17th century."

And before continuing to look at Franco's analysis of Salinger's nympholepsy, let's delve deeper into Salinger's "For Esmé—with Love and Squalor" and possibly gain some insight into why Franco choose this one story out of Salinger's *Nine Stories*.

In the short story, the protagonist, a member of the Army stationed in England, attended a children's choir practice where: "[…] girls, ranging in age from about seven to thirteen," were instructed to "open their mouths wider" and asked by their choir coach if they had: "[…] ever heard of a little dickeybird that dared to sing his charming song without first opening his little beak wide, wide, wide?" Subsequently, the choir coach: "[…] blew a note on her pitch pipe, and the children, like so many underage weightlifters, raised their hymnbooks." I would imagine that QAnon and his or her followers would have a field day with Salinger's paragraph, which has girls, ranging in ages from about 7 to 13, being instructed to open their mouths wider, before being asked if they had ever heard of a little *dick*eybird ahead of their choir coach blowing her pipe, which resulted in the nymphets raising their *hymn*books.[Emphasis mine.]

The soldier focused on Esmé whom he described as: "[…] about thirteen, with straight ash-blond hair of ear-lobe length, and exquisite forehead, and blasé eyes […]" And a "ladylike yawn" and "lovely" feet. After Esmé stared at the soldier and gave him a "qualified smile", she joined him at his table in the civilian tearoom where the soldier could see that Esmé was wearing a tartan dress that he opined was: "[…] a wonderful dress for a very young girl to be wearing on a rainy, rainy day."

Before "[s]he put her hands and wrists further forward on the table [...]", Esmé asked the soldier, "Are you very deeply in love with your wife? Or am I being too personal?"

Interestingly, while conversing with the soldier, Esmé toyed with her ash-blond hair, which any pickup artist will tell you is an IOI. "She quickly touched her hair again. 'Do you think you'll be coming here again in the immediate future?' she asked. 'We come her every Sunday, after choir practice.'"

Then the precocious nymphet asked, "Would you like me to write to you? I write extremely articulate letters for a person my—" Ultimately, Esmé bid the soldier adieu with a wave as she left the tearoom with her governess and even younger sibling.

Reviewing "For Esmé—with Love and Squalor" does give one some insight into why Franco, possibly misleadingly, opined that Salinger was obsessed with youth, but it may also give one some insight into why Franco chose to write about Esmé as well.

Here are some more misleading lines that Franco wrote about Salinger:

> According to Salerno and Shields, Salinger would be a companion to young women, real young women, for years, and then, according to pattern, one fateful night, he would sleep with them and the friendship would end. After that, after he'd fucked them, they were no longer the innocent ones running through the rye to be caught before they went over the cliff. They had gone over, and Salinger had been the one to push them.

This is pure hyperbole and, in some cases, simply not true. Firstly, which sentence from Salerno and Shields did Franco paraphrase to write: [...] after he'd fucked them, they were no longer the innocent one [...]". Secondly, *Oona O'Neill* left Salinger for Chaplin, Salinger married Claire Douglas, and Salinger never consummated his relationship with Joyce Maynard.

Alas, we've defended Salinger enough. Thus, let's discuss, of all people, Lindsay Lohan. Franco wrote: "Let's also remember that Lindsay, the Hollywood girl, is much younger than the Hollywood guy - probably underage when she met him back in the day, back in the club, Bungalow 8 in New York." After reading this, I re-read Franco's poems that were based on Lindsay Lohan - through a new lens. Interestingly, Lohan is peppered throughout Franco's oeuvre but highlighting some of the lines from "The Voice of Lindsay Lohan" may suffice.

Here are two lines from the first stanza: "This dragon girl, lion girl, Hollywood hellion, terro of Sunset Boulevard,*Minor in the clubs*, Chateau Demon?" [Emphasis mine.]

Then the voice of Lohan asked in a subsequent stanza: "How many young things selling movies, and wares,\\And music and tabloids fucked the kind of men I fucked?\\I was seventeen, eighteen, nineteen." This begs the question, "Why did Franco write that Lohan was "probably" underage when they met?" Well, if they met in LA, 17-year-old Lohan would have been "underage". But 17-year-old Lohan would have been "of age" in NYC.

And everyone knew it,

But they let me in their clubs,

They let me have their drugs,

They stuck their dicks in me,

And now Franco enters the picture. Per, "The Voice of Lindsay Lohan", *Lohan* took james into the bathroom so that he could "fuck' her, but since he didn't, she fucked a Greek man instead:

> I took James back to the bathroom.
> "You know why Amy puts mirrors
> All around here?"
> "Why?"
> "So that you can watch yourself fuck."
> He didn't fuck me, that shit.

> [...] I fucked one of the Greeks instead,
> A big-schnozzed, big-dicked,
> Drunk motherfucker.
> We did it in the bath.
> That was the best night of my [young] life.

"Mercution (Romeo's Right-Hand Man)" is in the chapter "Zeldra's Dreams" and appears to be based on Mercutio's speech in Shakespeare's *Romeo and Juliet*. This is Franco's first line: "I see Queen Mab, good Queen Mab, I do, I do. Do you?" And this is Mercutio's: "O, then, I see Queen Mab hath been with you." As you can see, they're very similar." Things change drastically in Franco's fourth stanza:

When I think of all the virgins I've taken

The clouds crack and bacon flashes, smell of bacon;

When I think of all the plays ever written I realize

There is nothing more expressive than a thigh being

bitten.

We've already reviewed that Juliet was a 13-year-old virgin at the beginning of *Romeo and Juliet,* but mentioning virgins reminds me of *Palo Alto*'s opening scene when Fred asked Teddy what he would do if he could go back in time. Teddy replied that he would be a king and fuck every virgin in his kingdom [like Augustus, the first emperor of the Roman Empire, whom we mentioned had "a passion for deflowering girls"].   Not to be biased, Franco mentioned another "nonvirgin" in the next paragraph: [...] Corine in a black trench, and white makeup...Corine, a nonvirgin at the age of thirteen [...]" However, Franco did not share who took the nymphet's virginity.

Let's stay with the nonvirgin theme but move to the next chapter - "The Actor Christmas" where Franco described Tosh Masuda who was: "[...] the crazy son of one of the richest men in the world [...]" Masuda suggested Roger who allowed *Katie* to seduce him to get revenge on her rich but reprehensible father. In Masuda's revenge story, he: "[...] legend has it, got a bad grade in history from a stiff teacher of moral rectitude, and then took out said teacher's daughter and then took her virginity. And then told him."

After Franco referenced his *New York Times* piece on selfies, he wrote about: "[...] the quarry, nestled in the Stanford

Hills, off of Old Page Mill Road; when we were in high school it was the place we'd go on nights there was no house to party in, as happens in *Dazed and Confused*."

Arguably, the most famous scene in *Dazed and Confused* (1993), a coming-of-age stoner comedy, is when David "Wood" Wooderson (Matthew McConaughey), related that, despite being in his twenties, he was considering going back to high school with his focus, not on procuring a belated high school diploma, but on procuring a high school coed. And not just any high school nymphet but the youngest - a freshman.

> Wood said, "Been thinkin' about gettin' back in school,
> man [...] That's where all the girls are, right?"
> Wood asked, "Say, you're a freshman, right?"
> Freshman: "Yeah."
> "So, tell me man. How's this year's crop of freshman
> chicks lookin'?"
> "Wood, you're gonna end up in jail sometime really soon."
> After a head turning high school girl passed, Wood
> revealed, "That's what I love about these high school girls,
> man. I get older, they stay the same age. Yes, they do."

We can infer that Chaplin, Woody, and Salinger would (openly) concur with Wood. And, based on my research, I would argue that most men would (secretly) concur with Wood. How does the saying go? It's something like, "When you're 14, you're attracted to high school girls, and when you're 41, you're <u>still</u> attracted to high school girls."

Back in the quarry, the narrator of "The Actor Christmas" wrote about one night when he was still too young to get his driver's license, he went to the quarry with Max Meerbaum - his high school idol, and two girls - Alice and her pretty, privileged, and nice friend. The narrator was shocked that Max asked Alice if she wanted to do 69. "Fuck, out in the wilderness?"

The narrator got into a fight with Sam Miller near their elementary school lockers. Consequently, Sam's sister, Bedpost, sent two junior high school boys to beat up the narrator. Her name: "[...] was Bedpost, because she once grabbed a bedpost, bent over, and said to her boyfriend, *Fuck me, fuck me* [...]" It's not clear when Sam's sister got the nickname Bedpost, but it happened sometime between birth and high school.

Remember Mr. DeFelice's, the narrator's elementary school teacher from *Palo Alto: Stories,* who asked to take photographs of Simone, a pretty and blonde like Madonna fourth grader, but her mother refused the teacher's request? Well, it turns out that Mr. DeAmo, the narrator's seventh grade teacher, was a bit of an amateur photographer [of nymphets]. To the narrator's dismay, Mr. DeAmo asked Nicole, the narrator's former elementary school girlfriend: "[...] to pose for pictures, alone, like a little Marilyn Monroe at age ten, on the Hoover Park playground [...]"

On the next page, Franco revealed that: "[...] Roberto [is] the name I gave the real guy in my book *Palo Alto.*" Remember, in *Palo Alto,* Emily shared that Ryan wasn't: "[...] like the assholes in my grade like Adam and Roberto who just wanted to fuck and do it in the ass. Or come on my face like a porn star [...]" Sadly, Franco didn't have Emily state what grade she was in when Adam and

Roberto wanted to come on her face. But we can infer that, like Bedpost, it was sometime between birth and high school.

The narrator in "Seventh Grade" was intimidated by his new Black and Brown schoolmates whom he, to put it mildly, assumed had:

> [...] dicks so big they could kill you [...] Gemal and Shaka
> and Ramone and Ruben,
> They are different kinds of people than you have ever
> known.
> The halls are full of these people and talk about pussy and
> guns
> And a girl named Yvon who sucked Shaka's dick [in
> "Seventh Grade"]

In "Her", Franco opined: "And then there was [...] Hepburn [in] things like *B'fast at T's*, which I didn't know at the time was a butchering of the novella - a *straight* stand-in for Capote!"

I would have to agree with Franco, because *Breakfast at Tiffany's* (1961) made no mention of the fact that in the Capote's novella, Holiday Golightly married a much older man at the age of thirteen. She lived with a college jock at the age of fifteen. And at the age of eighteen, Golightly stated, "I can't get excited by a man until he's at least forty-two."

In "Because", Franco reiterated what he shared with Howard Stern about his fans being "[...] fucking fourteen-year-olds."

> Because I played a knight,
>
> And was on a screen,
>
> Because I made a million dollars,
>
> Because I was handsome,
>
> Because I had a nice car,
>
> A bunch of girls seemed to like me.
>
> [...] Liked me, and shit, they were all fucking fourteen-year olds.

In "Editing", Franco referenced *Paranoid Park* (2007):

> […] In *Paranoid Park* there is this
>
> Punk girl that [*sic*] keeps looking straight into
>
> The camera when she speaks,
>
> It's like she's speaking to us.

It appears that Franco was referring to Jennifer whom was played by 13-year-old Taylor Momsen. Alex, an avid skateboarder, said, "Jennifer was nice and everything, but she was a virgin, which meant she'd want to do it at some point." And she did. An hour into the film, which is about Alex's involvement in the manslaughter of a railway security guard, Jennifer guided Alex by the hand through the house's two car garage and up the carpeted stairs before she removed his t-shirt, pushed him onto the bed, peppered him with kisses and made love to him in the cowgirl position while their high school classmates frolicked in the backyard pool.

"[…] Amazing! Do you think we should do it again? Or maybe we should wait?" Jennifer asked. They waited, but as Jennifer put on her *petit* bra, she said, "You know. We're gonna need more condoms. We should go to Rite Aid and get them […]" They didn't go, but Jennifer called a friend and exclaimed, "Yeah, we totally did it. Oh my God! I know right? No, it was fantastic!"

Paranoid Park (2007) is closely based on Blake Nelson's novel of the same name; thus, the teen sex scenes between Alex and Jennifer are very similar in the film and in the novel except for some notable differences. For example, I learned in the novel that Jennifer's last name was Hasselbach. And that she was "hot", "cute", had "beautiful long blonde hair", and that she was a varsity cheerleader. Being a member of the varsity cheerleader squad put Jennifer in, at a minimum, the 11th grade (i.e., approximately 16-years-old). The novel related that Alex was a 16-year-old junior; thus, it makes sense that Alex was played by (approximately) 16-year-old Gabe Nevins in the film. But why was 13-year-old Taylor Momsen chosen to play Jennifer?

It turns out that one of the reasons Jennifer wanted to lose her virginity was for competitive reasons. Petra, Jennifer's schoolmate, despite having only gone out with Mike Paley for a couple of weeks, did it with him: "[…] three times last weekend." "And Maddy did it last summer." Consequently, at Christian Barlow's Friday night house party, around midnight, Jennifer grabbed Alex by hand, pulled him upstairs to a "little girl's" bedroom, locked the door, put her arms around Alex while appearing to be "wild with passion", and, just like in the film, Jennifer had teen sex with Alex in the cowgirl position while the other high schoolers partied downstairs. And just like in the film, Jennifer asked Alex if he wanted to do it again or wait, and Jennifer reminded Alex that they were going to need more condoms. In the novel, Jennifer critiqued Alex's sexual performance: "You were so good," she sighed. "Was I good?" Alex's response? "Yes." And just like in the film, Jennifer called a friend to exclaim that her sex with Alex was "*fantastic*".

In "Chateau Dreams", Franco referenced Lindsay Lohan again, and he referenced Nick Ray's age-gap affair with Natalie Wood:

> In '82, John Belushi died from a speedball in Bungalow 3;
> In '54, forty-three-year-old Nick Ray
> Fucked fifteen-year-old Natalie Wood in Bungalow 2;
> In 2005, Lindsay Lohan lived in room 19 for two years
> Because "she didn't want to be alone."
> Ambulance calls were the regular antidote to her demon
> nights

Sam Kashner related in "Dangerous Talents" – a *Vanity Fair* piece:

> Natalie Wood desperately wanted the part [in *Rebel Without a Cause* (1955)], but at 16 she had played only juveniles [...] Ray [the film's director] was immediately drawn to Wood, Gavin Lambert recalls. "She was very young, and that was always attractive to Nick," he says [...] "How quickly did Natalie realize that he found her extremely desirable, and

how soon did Nick make his move? … The interview took place in the first week of February, and by the time she made her first screen test, ten days later they were lovers," recalls Lambert.

Wood's affair with Ray awakened her sexuality—and emboldened her to initiate another love affair, this one with Dennis Hopper, who had been cast as Goon. "I was astonished," Hopper later said. "I came from a very conventional, middle-class family in San Diego … and this was the 1950s, when girls who'd turned sixteen only a few months earlier just didn't do things like that." The sexually charged situation created ill will between Ray and Hopper.

Franco wrote that Wood was 15, but Kashner wrote that she was 16. I don't know Franco's source, but Hopper may have clarified the issue by sharing that when he began his affair with the nymphet she had "turned sixteen only a few months earlier". That supports Franco's position, because it could take months for a film to start shooting after a "screen test".

Only God knows how many nymphets had sex in the infamous Chateau Marmont, but *Daily Mail*'s Glenys Roberts related in "The real Hotel Babylon: A new film tells how the Chateau Marmont became a byword for Hollywood debauchery":

A 19-year-old Scarlett Johansson was so overcome by its heady atmosphere in 2004 that she couldn't wait to get upstairs with [thirty-seven-year-old] Puerto Rican star -

Benicio Del Toro and ripped off his clothes in the lift. 'We were making out or having sex or something,' she readily admitted later."

One may not infer from Franco's title that "Ask" is about (pre)teen sex. More specifically, it's about having sex immediately after reaching puberty - even if one has to have sex with an ugly partner:

> With girls
> Just push and it gets there.
> As soon as you hit puberty, go.
> Take what comes, ugly is okay too.

Franco wrote about You whom had sex: "With Erica, you were on someone's brothers bed;" Erica asked You to be: "*Gentle,* but you weren't.*" Instead, You had an (pre)teen orgasm via a number of thrusts: "Love came - like viscosity filling a tube -\And you killed it with a bunch of thrusts." And it appears that Erica considered having her virginity taken by You as a rite of passage:

> *In the bathroom I sat naked on the floor.*
> *Blood blooming.*
> *-Science* and *fiction.*
> *This is the rite of passage.*
> *I am the vessel.*
> *He is the instrument.*

In "Stop Me If You Think That You've Heard This One Before", Franco put seventh graders into three categories: kids who played football, kings who got great grades, and "[...] others that danced among us." But it wasn't clear which category of seventh graders Franco was referring to when he composed in the next stanza: "They were big, daring, and sexual." However, in general, it's clear that Franco considered a category of seventh graders to be sexual, which is in tune with Judith Levine's *Harmful to Minors: The Perils of Protecting Children From Sex"*. In the 2002 *Los Angeles Times* Book Prize winner, Levine wrote:

> [...] fear about child sexuality stems from two sources: feminists and the Christian religious Right: The political articulation of these fears in the late twentieth century came from two disparate sources.
>
> 1. On one side were feminists, whose movement exposed widespread rape and domestic sexual violence against women and children and initiated a new body of law (e.g., age of consent) that would punish the perpetrator and cease to blame the victim.
>
> 2. From the other side, the religious Right brought to sexual politics the belief that women and children need special protection because they are "naturally" averse to sex of any kind.

Levine wrote that approximately 50% of nymphets between the ages of 15 and 19 are sexually active. And that:

> In the 1950s, plenty of teens had sex, but it wasn't considered troublesome because it wasn't premarital: in

that decade, America had the highest rate of teen marriage in the Western world." Currently, approximately 90% of heterosexual Americans have sexual intercourse before marriage.

Levine wrote that experts give a variety of reasons for teen sex but fail to mention that teens have sex because, simply, sex feels good:

> In almost every article or broadcast, experts are called in to catalogue the reasons that teens have sex, all of them bad: Their peers pressure them or pedophiles manipulate them; they drink or drug too much, listen to rap, or download porn; they are under too much pressure or aren't challenged enough; they are abused or abusive or feel immortal or suicidal; they're rich and spoiled or poor and demoralized, raised too strictly or too permissively; they are ignorant or oversophisticated.
>
> Squeamish or ignorant about facts, parents appear to accept the pundits' worst conjectures about their children's sexual motives. It's as if they cannot imagine that their kids seek sex for the same reasons they do: They like or love the person they are having it with. It gives them a sense of beauty, worthiness, happiness, or power. And it feels good.

Levine reiterated the notion that assuming that teen sex is perilous is a perilous way of thinking:

Indeed, the concept that sex poses an almost existential peril to children, that it robs them of their very childhood, was born only about 150 years ago.

According to the influential French historian Philippe Ariès, European societies before the eighteenth century did not recognize what we now call childhood, defined as a long period of dependency and protection lasting into physical and social maturity.

Levine even opined that protecting minors from sex is harmful:

> Harmful to Minors launches from two negatives: sex is not ipso facto harmful to minors; and America's drive to protect kids from sex is protecting them from nothing.

> Instead, often it is harming them. [...] adults owe children not only protection and a schooling in safety but also the entitlement to pleasure.

Lastly, at almost 300 pages, *Harmful to Minors* is full of interesting facts and anecdotes about teen sexuality e.g.:

> 1. Sherry Turkle of MIT shared: "A 13-year-old informs me that she prefers to do her sexual experimentation online. Her partners are usually the boys in her class at

school. In person, she says, it is 'mostly grope-y.' Online, 'they need to talk more.'"

2. A major longitudinal study at UCLA found that 75% of kids had masturbated and/or had sex with another child before the age of six.

3. "Psychologists Sharon Lamb and Mary Coakley surveyed three hundred psychologically healthy Bryn Mawr students about their childhood sexual experiences. The young women wrote about thrilling games of porn star, prostitute, rape, and slave girl, all at ages in the single digits [...]"

4. Joan Rappaport led "Adolescent Issues", a series of discussions at a Manhattan private school where she gave her sixth-grade students the homework assignment: "Go home and find your clitorises."

5. And "Flora masturbated at six or seven and had orgasms starting at ten or eleven. When she was that age, a thirteen-year-old friend joined her. 'We would lay around and take off our clothes,' Flora recalled [...] We even made dildos out of toilet paper and Vaseline.' She recounted the story without shame or regret: in fact, she spoke with glee."

Thus, it appears that Franco knew what he was talking about when he wrote about (pre)teen sex.

I have never been to Disneyland, I'm a Coney Island guy, but if I had been to Disneyland, maybe I would have known that, per "Splash Mountain", boys: "[...] fingered girls in the Haunted House."

In "This Charming Man", at age 12, Tom rode his bicycle over the bike bridge to school. By 15, he tried "it" in the back of a car with Sharon. At 16, Tom: "[...] had the love life of the octopus,\Groping and grappling," But at: "Age fourteen, fifteen, sixteen, seventeen,\Erica was *with* Sterling" [Emphasis mine]

How about some more adolescent voyeurism from "Reel around the Fountain":

In the parking lot,

In the 'stang,

After school,

Before his practice,

They kissed, hard.

Lips to lips,

Sharp teeth to sheep teeth, A ritual.

Everyday, from then on,

I would watch

Herbert White (2010), *Directing Herbert White* (2014), and "Directing Herbert White" are arguably Franco's most controversial nympholepsy themed pieces as they fall into what I have deemed, for lack of a better non-racist phrase, the dark side of nympholepsy, which is what happens when men, unlike Elvis and Charlie Chaplin, decide not to marry nymphets but resort to teen porn, teen prostitution, incest, (non-statutory) rape and in even murder.

As you see, Franco was so, what's the word, intrigued by Frank Bidart's poem "Herbert White" that he wrote and directed a (short) film based on the poem, Franco published a book with the poem's title, <u>and</u> Franco penned a poem about the poem. #meta

Let's begin by sharing some excerpts from Bidart's "Herbert White", which is about a married, with kids, serial killer who kidnaped nymphets and raped them - even after death. And when the nymphet's bodies became too decomposed for necrophilia, Herbert White masturbated "letting it fall on her":

When I hit her on the head, it was good,

and then I did it to her a couple of times,—[...] I liked to

drive past the woods where she lay,

tell the old lady and the kids I had to take a piss,

hop out and do it to her... [...] When the body got too

discomposed,

I'd just jack off, letting it fall on her…[...] well, like I said,

she didn't move: and I saw,

under me, a little girl was just lying there in the mud: [...] I

got in the truck, and started to drive,

and saw a [new] little girl—

who I picked up, hit on the head, and

screwed, and screwed, and screwed, and screwed, then

buried,

in the garden of the motel…[...] —About six months ago,

I heard Dad remarried,

so I drove over to Connecticut to see him and see

if he was happy.

She was twenty-five years younger than him: [...] I kept

thinking about getting a [new] girl,

and the more I thought I shouldn't do it,

the more I had to—

I saw her coming out of the movies,

saw she was alone, and

kept circling the

blocks as she walked along them,

saying, 'You're going to leave her alone.'

'You're going to leave her alone.'

Except for the part where the serial killer visited his father, whom married a woman "twenty-five years younger than him", Franco's *Herbert White* (2010) depicted Bidart's poem very closely; thus, let us take a look at Franco's poem "Directing Herbert White" where we learn that Bidart, a Pulitzer Prize winning poet, wrote "Herbert White" while he was a student at Harvard and that Herbert White is based on "The Necrophiliac" - a medical case study in *21 Abnormal Sex Cases*.

Franco wrote that after he heard the poem read in class at Warren Wilson College, he recognized that he wanted to adapt the poem. "These impulses are visceral." Yes. The allure of nymphets does cause some men to have visceral impulses. Yet for some reason, Franco wrote: "Herbert has a secret - he's a murderer of women and a fucker of corpses - which he can tell no one," instead of: "Herbert has a secret - he's a murderer of nymphets and a fucker of teen corpses - which he can tell no one." However, going back to the work ethic motif, Franco disclosed, of Bidart: "He lives alone among stacks of books and DVDs and CDs. The stacks are so large and numerous they have become his walls."

Twilight, teen vampires and the Beat Generation reappears in "New Rebel", which is the tenth poem in *Straight James/Gay James* (2015):

> Shot through the vampire teen phenomenon of Robert Pattinson,
> and even more so in his hard core ex, Kristen Stewart, a brooding Dean if I ever saw one.
> Shot through Jack Kerouac and Neal Cassady out on the road.

Since we have previously elaborated on *Twilight*, Kerouac and Cassady, let's elaborate on Stewart.

Talk about art imitating life, Kristen Stewart, twenty-two, and Robert Pattinson, twenty-six, developed a relationship on the set of the *Twilight* series that continued over the years until Kristen began an affair on the set of *Snow White and the Huntsman* with Rupert Sandars, the forty-one-year-old married director of the film.

We've written more than twice that in Kerouac's *On The Road*, Dean (Neal Cassady) reminisced about a three-day liaison in the Ace Hotel with 15-year-old Marylou, but guess who played Marylou in the film adaptation of the novel? You guessed it, Kristen Stewart.

In subsequent stanzas in "New Rebel", Franco composed:

The Bling Ringers, those teens who stole all that shit from Lindsay Lohan, and Paris Hilton, they are punk rockers of today [...]

The Bling Ringers are pretty, but they're criminals. They're MTV on the surface, and Sid Vicious underneath.

One of the pretty Bling Ringers was Alexis Neier, who was on *Pretty Wild* (2010) - an E! reality show. From NBC's About the Show:

> "Pretty Wild" follows the lives of sisters Tess Taylor [19-years-old] and Alexis [18-years-old] and Gabrielle Neiers [15-years-old] and their unconventional Hollywood family. The series presents an unfiltered look at Hollywood from the perspective of the *[teen] sisters* whose *jaw-dropping looks* and unstructured upbringing make them *magnets for those who have fallen for Tinseltown's many temptations.* [Emphasis mine]

Richard Lawson wrote a review of the reality show for *Gawker*:

> The girls have a stripper pole installed in the house and regularly use it, to the delight of their mother. (And possibly the step-father.) [And] [...] the mom gives out Adderall to her girls every morning like vitamins [...] They play up the sexy theatrics so much — because ridiculous shit like that gets good ratings [...] That said, you simply have to watch it. [...] It's really something.

I followed Lawson's advice and streamed *Pretty Wild* on the NBC app on my iPhone and in addition to the prominent and recurring (teen) stripper pole, Alexis and Tess were filmed repeatedly in the nude - although very slightly blurred. In one scene, in episode 8, Mrs. Arlington, the nymphet's mother, informed Tess, "No one has breasts like you do. They are phenomenal!" Subsequently, Mrs. Arlington photographed a nude Tess in the family shower.

It turns out that Tess was a family friend who the Neiers considered an adopted sister, which is comforting as Tess had a habit of kissing Alexis - on the lips and touching Alexis' teen fountains and mountains.

And Alexis was an (open) teleiophile. For example, in episode 3, Alexis unzipped her top and posed seductively for the movers. Mrs. Arlington asked, "Why are you doing this? For the movers? I hope not." Alexis, "They're cute." In episode 4, after a man passed her in the supermarket, Alexis asked, "Is that a DILF? Dad I'd like to bang (i.e., fuck)." And in episode 8, Alexis advised Tess, "Max is a cute boy. Josh is a real man." In addition, in episode 1, before Tess walked in the lingerie fashion show in a thong, the designer advised, "Make sure you remember to flirt with those photographers." (As an interesting side note, Alexis revealed on Vice's *Alexis Neiers on Drugs, Prison, and the Bling Ring: Profiles*, that she had a $10,000 drug habit while filming *Pretty Wild* and that she started swallowing Xanax in 7th grade and snorting cocaine and meth in the 8th grade!)

My initial sources for nympholepsy in pop culture were "highbrow" publications such as *Vanity Fair, New York Magazine, The New Yorker,* and the *New York Times*. But most recently, I have benefited from social media. For example, Comments by Celebs posted a screenshot from Paris Hilton's Instagram account. This is what I posted on *The Allure of Nymphets* blog:

> For #FBF [Flash Back Friday] (APRIL 24, 2020), Paris Hilton was apparently filled with nostalgia. Consequently, she posted a seductive photo on her Instagram (IG) account from when she was a 15-year-old nymphet. In the photo, a nubile Hilton's derriere is barely covered by her skimpy skirt, her young but large breasts are prominent, and her look is flirtatious. Hilton wrote in the caption that she used a push up bra to help prominently display her fountains: "Back when I was 15 and discovered the wonders of a push up bra and eyeliner." As of the time of this post, Hilton's IG post was viewed 3,001,800 times, and it had over 3,000 comments such as from mr.gus.bridges who wrote: "You Derty lil girl"

Subsequently, Emma Diamond and Julie Kramer, the Comments by Celebs podcasters, devoted a segment to *This Is Paris* (2020) - Paris Hilton's documentary. Consequently, I streamed *This Is Paris* (2020) and was shocked to learn that *1 Night in Paris* (2004), Paris' (in)famous sex tape, was filmed when she was 18. And Rick Salomon, her co-star slash boyfriend, was in his early thirties. Paris documented, "That was a private moment with a teenage girl." And, "It was my first real relationship - 18. I was just so in love with him. I wanted to make him happy."

Like Lindsay Lohan, Lana Del Rey is (lightly) peppered throughout Franco's written oeuvre. For example, in "Lana Poem Essay", Franco wrote:

> This is a poem about Lana Del Rey.
> This is an essay about Lana Del Rey.
> Lana has become my friend. She is a musician who is a poet and a video artist.
> When I watch her stuff, when I listen to her stuff, I am reminded of everything I love about Los Angeles [...] The only difference between Lana and me is her haunting voice. That carries everything. The voice is the central axle around which the spokes of everything else extend.

Interestingly, Lana is a fan of *Lolita* - so much so that references to the most famous nymphet are peppered throughout Lana's lyrics. And in Malka Howley's PopMatters article, "You Know You Like Little Girls: Lana Del Rey and Dolores Haze", Lana Del Rey described herself as, "Lolita lost in the hood."

Thus, unsurprisingly, references to the most famous nymphet are peppered throughout Lana's early lyrics. For example, "Little Girls (Put Me In A Movie)" is a song on *Lana Del Ray* (2010). Here is a self-explanatory excerpt from the lyrics:

> Lights, camera, action
> If he likes me, takes me home
> Come on, you know you like little girls
> Come on, you know you like little girls

You can be my daddy

You can be my daddy

What may not be apparent is that "Put Me In A Movie" is an additional reference to *Lolita* as Lolita had an affinity for the movies. "Everything was fine. There, in the lobby, she [Lolita] sat, deep in an overstuffed blood-red armchair, deep in a lurid movie magazine."

"Carmen" is a song that was co-written by Lana and is on *Born to Die* (2012) - Lana's second album. Sometimes, Humbert referred to Lolita as Carmen. "My Carmen," I said (I used to call her that sometimes), "we shall leave this raw sore town as soon as you get out of bed."

"Off to the Races" is on *Born to Die* too and was co-written by Lana as well. A riff of "Off to the Races" is based on one of Lolita's most famous sentences:

Light of his life, fire of his loins

Keep me forever, tell me you want me

Light of your life, fire of your loins

Tell me you want me, gimme them coins

Humbert said it better: "Lolita, light of my life, fire of my loins. My sin, my soul. Lo-lee-ta: the tip of the tongue taking a trip of three steps down the palate to tap, at three, on the teeth. Lo. Lee. Ta."

And "Lolita" is on *Born to Die: The Paradise Edition* (2012) - an album reissue. Here is "Lolita's" riff:

Hey Lolita, hey

Hey Lolita, hey

I know what the boys want, I'm not gonna play

Hey Lolita, hey

Hey Lolita, hey

Whistle all you want but I'm not gonna say

No more skipping rope, skipping heart beats with the boys

downtown

Just you and me feeling the heat even when the sun goes

down

It turns out that, in addition to Lana, Franco is an admirer of *Lolita,* which is evidenced by Franco's Instagram post of *Lolita* sunbathing on the beach with the caption: "Reading mah [*sic*] favorite book on the beach. LO-LI-Ta" Franco is a well-known avid reader with a BA in English from UCLA, a MFA from Columbia University, and he may or may not still be working on a PhD from Yale; thus, it's significant that, out of all the books that he has read and perused, *Lolita* is admittedly his very favorite.

Here's *Lolita*'s plot summary from *Nymphalis Carmen: Nympholepsy in Nabokov's Oeuvre*:

Humbert Humbert (H.H.), a middle-aged literature professor, is enticed by Dolores "Lolita" Haze, a twelve-year-old nymphet. Humbert strategically marries Lolita's mother and after the mother dies, Humbert takes his nymphet on a road trip where they begin a sexual affair, but Lolita's secret sexual affair with Quilty, a playwright and fellow nympholept, ends badly for Humbert and Quilty.

I related in *Nymphalis Carmen* that in a *Rookie* magazine article for teens, "Older Men: Everything You Always Wanted to Know about Them, and Weren't at All Afraid to Ask.", Amy Rose Spiegel misleadingly wrote that *Lolita*, a novel that Spiegel "romanticized" as a nymphet, was a: "[...] story about an adult man kidnapping, molesting, and raping an adolescent girl". However, as we wrote earlier, novelist Robertson Davies' assessment of the book as "[...] not [about] the corruption of an innocent child by a cunning adult, but [about] the exploitation of a weak adult by a corrupt child" may be more accurate.

But what is it about *Lolita* that fascinates Spiegel, Lana, Franco and millions of other readers? Is it the age-gap love triangle between Humbert, Lolita, and Quilty? Or is it the additional nympholepsy that's peppered throughout *Lolita*. Who knows? But for the non-pedantic reader, let's share only three examples of the additional nympholepsy in the Nabokov's most famous and favorite novel.

1. Nabokov stated in a 1967 *Wisconsin Studies in Contemporary Literature* (vol. III, no. 2) interview with Alfred Appel that of all his novels, he held the greatest affection for *Lolita* and, unsurprisingly, the nympholepsy motif appears almost immediately in the novel.

The beginning of the third sentence: "Lo-lee-ta […]" gives the readers their first allusion to nympholepsy. (9) Alfred Appel Jr, wrote in the notes to *The Annotated Lolita*: "[…] the middle syllable alludes to [Poe's] "Annabel Lee" (1949) […]"

Interestingly, Poe is alluded to over twenty times in the *Lolita*. And that the apparent connections between Humbert and Poe are their "child brides". (330) Nabokov elaborates on page forty-three: "Virginia was not quite fourteen when Harry Edgar possessed her. He gave her lessons in algebra. *Je m'imagine cela*. They spent their honeymoon at Petersburg, Fla." Appel noted that Poe was twenty-seven when he married, *à la* Jerry Lee Lewis, Virginia Clemm, his thirteen-year-old cousin.

2. H.H. describes a wall painting of "pre-nubile" nude Neferneferure and Neferneferuaten, two daughters of King Akhnaten and Queen Nefertiti, and 10-year-old brides straddling fascinum (i.e., ivory dildos):

"Here is Virgil who could the nymphet sing in single tone […] Here are two of King Akhnaten's and Queen Nefertiti's pre-nubile Nile daughters (that royal couple had a litter of six), wearing nothing but many necklaces of bright beads, relaxed on cushions, intact after three thousand years, with their soft brown puppybodies, cropped hair and long ebony eyes. Here are some brides of ten compelled to seat themselves on the fascinum, the virile ivory in the temples of classical scholarship."

3. Before Lolita rested her legs on Hubert's lap, she showed him a picture in a magazine:

"[…] a surrealist painter relaxing, supine, on a beach, and near him, likewise supine, a plaster replica of the Venus di Milo, half-buried in sand. Picture of the Week, said the legend.

Maurice Couturier wrote in *Nabokov's Eros and the Poetics of Desire*: "The whole scene, rather the photo itself, may point towards another painting, *L'Impromptu de Versailles*, painted by Magritte in 1933 to illustrate a book entitled *Violette Nozière*: it shows a grown-up man sitting on a chair and holding a young girl on his knees whom he strokes under her dress; facing him, there is another man with a solemn face, a top hat, holding a leather briefcase under his arm who looks like a syncretic representation of Freud and the painter." (270) *Violette Nozière* is about eighteen-year-old Violette Nozière who poisoned her parents, because her father had been allegedly molesting her since she was twelve. The 1978 film adaptation of the 1933 true-crime portrayed Nozière as a teleiophile who had a number of affairs with older men.

As of the writing of this book, *Straight James Gay James* is Franco's last published book and the last poem in his last (poetry) book is "Bildungsromans and Bildungsromans" where Franco fittingly concludes with two stanzas about "the sweetest" high school bodies having "the best" sex:

> High school is ages
>
> Fourteen to eighteen,
>
> When puberty hits its stride
>
> And bodies are the sweetest.
>
> Sex in high school
>
> Is the most forbidden,
>
> And I think the best,
>
> The participants don't know the moves

In subsequent stanzas, Franco name dropped a number of famous creative types such as Stephen King, Harmony Korine (again), Larry Clark, Richard Prince, and Sofia Coppola.

E. Alex Jung's *Vulture* piece "How Does the New *It* Movie Deal With Stephen King's [Pre-teen] Orgy Scene?" related:

> Since its publication in September of 1986, *It* has enjoyed a long shelf life, first as a book that spent 14 weeks at the top of the *New York Times* best-seller list [...] This week, *It* hits theaters for the first time as a feature film [...].

> But one controversial scene from King's novel has dogged the book and subsequent adaptations. After defeating *It*,

the kids get lost in the sewer tunnels on the way out; this is attributed in part to the fact that they're losing their "connection" to one another. The solution is to bind them together, which Beverly — the only girl in the story's main group of protagonists, called "the Losers" — says can only happen if each of the boys has sex with her. Where they're timid and unsure, she's confident and maternal [...] The sex is a "consensual" gang bang, with each of the boys losing his virginity, and thus entering manhood, through Beverly.

[...] critics and readers looking back at it have called it everything from "disturbing" to "sick" to "insane." A Reddit reader from last year simply asked, "WTF?" and generated over 500 comments. For almost ten exhaustive pages, King describes each of the boys having sex with Beverly and their orgasms as a version of "flying."

Here are two relevant excerpts from Stephen King's *It*:

"You have to put your thing in me."

"Mike comes to her, then Richie, and the act is repeated. Now she feels some pleasure, dim heat in her childish unmatured sex, and she closes her eyes as Stan comes to her and she thinks of the birds."

Although, Beverly doesn't have sex in the film adaptation, Jung related that the film: "[...] sexualizes her several times, like when she flirts with a middle-aged cashier at a pharmacy to help the boys steal some supplies."

This is IMDb's plot summary for Larry Clark's *Kids* (1995): "A day in the life of a group of teens as they travel around New York City skating, drinking, smoking and deflowering virgins." And this is how one Jewish *Kids* described, in a strong New York accent, how he "deflowered" a virgin:

> "Yo, you know what else? You can tell she just ended puberty […] I was like, oh shit yo, this girl's a baby […] that turns me on. I wanna fuck this little baby girl [...] When I was fucking her, I kept thinking about how much I wanted to put it in her ass dud".

Oh, and by the way, Larry Clark may have directed *Kids* (1995), but the coming-of-age exploitation film was written by our very own Harmony Korine.

Like *The Tenants*' Harry Lesser, I am a frequent visitor of art museums; however, if there is a relevant exhibit, I will dip into a snooty art gallery in Chelsea. And on one such occasion, I went to view the Disturbing Innocence exhibit at the The FLAG Art Foundation where I saw John Wesley's *Caryn and Robin* (1968), Steve Gianakos' *The Farm Had Been Rescinded Just A Month Earlier* (2011), and Richard Prince's *Spiritual America* (1983).

Wesley's *Caryn and Robin* (1968) depicts two prepubescent girls in a lipstick lesbian erotic pose. Chris Bors of *Art Voices* wrote that Gianakos' *The Farm Had Been Rescinded Just A Month Earlier*

(2011): "[...] depicts a girl with Kewpie doll style eyes reverse straddling a line of pigs that are eating out of a trough, while getting stimulated by one of their tails as a bird, cat and rooster look on."

And Prince's *Spiritual America* (1983) is a photograph of 10-year-old Brooke Shields – in the nude.

In addition to the The FLAG Art Foundation, Prince's *Spiritual America* had been exhibited at the Guggenheim museum. And if you have any questions about whether or not the exhibit was of a sexual nature, consider the fact that none other than the Playboy Press paid Brooke's mother $450 for the photograph. The press release for the exhibit stated:

> For Prince, this troubling image and its controversial history encapsulates the dueling impulses at the heart of the American psyche, with its overarching puritan ethics countered by a yearning for recognition, even at the price of transgression and degradation.

I'm not sure what that means, but the press release was saying something about the battle between having morals and the need for attention - even if the need for attention causes one to transgress his or her morals and stoop to the level of degradation. To some, that is exactly what Prince did by exhibiting a photograph of a nude "prepubescent Brooke Shields posing in a brothel-like atmosphere, [with] her face made up like a grown woman's." And prior to the Guggenheim exhibit, Prince exhibited the nude nymphet at an art studio on the Lower East Side.

Not to be outdone by the Guggenheim, the MoMA's *Talk To Me* exhibit afforded me the opportunity to view a semi-nude photograph of a seductively posing 10-year-old Brook Shields. And I viewed the half-nude nymphet while (virtually) flipping through an issue of Olivier Zahm's *Purple* magazine.

In the *Purple* spread, which was shot by the previously mentioned infamous photographer Terry Richardson, the actress Chloe Sevigny was photographed in a black satin floor length slim dress and a white sleeveless blouse as she stood on a plush brown rug in front of two nude photographs of ten-year-old Brooke Shields. In one photograph, Brooke's buttocks were in clear view as she smelled a yellow flower. In the other photograph, despite copious amounts of makeup, her nude physique clearly revealed that she was an early nymphet.

In our discussion of Franco's "New Rebel", I failed to mention that Sofia Coppola directed and co-wrote *The Bling Ring* (2013), which is based on Alexis Neier and the Bling Ring but Franco's Sofia Coppola name drop in "Bildungsromans and Bildungsromans" reminded me of *Somewhere* (2010).

Read IMDb's plot summary of *Somewhere,* which Sofia Coppola directed and wrote: "After withdrawing to the Chateau Marmont, a passionless Hollywood actor [Johnny Marco (Stephen Dorff)] reexamines his life when his eleven-year-old daughter surprises him with a visit."

In two scenes in the film, Marco hires Bambi and Cindy, two strippers, to entertain him in his Chateau Marmont room. Bambi and Cindy were played by Kristina Shannon and Karissa Shannon, respectively - The Shannon Twins. Two years prior to the release of *Somewhere,* the 19-year-old twins moved into the Playboy Mansion and became two of Hugh Hefner's girlfriends. How old was Hef, you may ask? He was in his early eighties.

And with that we conclude our discussion of Franco's written oeuvre, but before concluding this chapter, let's take a look at a number of Franco's films. For example, here's *Pineapple Express'* (2008) Movie Info from Rotten Tomatoes:

> Critically acclaimed director David Gordon Green takes a break [...] for this action-flavored buddy comedy concerning two pot-smoking friends (Seth Rogen and James Franco) who unwittingly become involved with a vicious gang of drug dealers. Judd Apatow and Shauna Robertson produce a script co-penned by star Rogen and Evan Goldberg.

In the film, Dale Denton (Seth Rogen) shared with KRAD talk radio:

> Dale: "I'm just saying love has no age. You can't instantly tell me that a man, because he's a certain age can't marry a [much younger] woman or love a [much younger] woman. I'm dating a high school girl [...] if I'm 25 and the girl is 18-years-old you know in society that might look bad."
> Talk radio host: "Hey, as long as it's consensual."
> Dale: "I think it's consensual."

Subsequently, during his lunch break, Dale visited Angie, his teen girlfriend, at her high school. Consequently, a teacher asked Dale why he didn't date someone his own age, and Dale responded, "She's very mature for her age."

After visiting Angie, Dale visited Saul (James Franco) and expressed with Saul that he feels like a, "[...] fat, dumb, fucking stinky ass-turd" around Angie's, "[...] strong and handsome and really funny" classmates. Saul encouraged, "You know, don't get down on yourself. You got a great girl." However, Dale told Angie, "[...] you are gonna go to college next year [...] And you'll blow a bunch of dudes and become a lesbian, and I'll be here in fucking Clark County doing shit-all. You're gonna dump me. So, fuck it, have a good time." [Note: Dale related that he and Angie had been dating for three months, and Dale stated that Angie would be going to college "next year". That implies that they met during the first semester of Angie's senior year of high school, which would imply that they met when Angie was 17.]

Later, Dale regretted what he said and cried, "Angie, I'm calling, because I love you more than anything in the world and I wanna let you know I'll do anything to make it work [...] I love you." Angie: "I love you [...] I wanna marry you"

But Dale didn't want to get married and told Angie that she was immature for not realizing that he was a "fuck-up". Angie responded by confessing, "I'm not immature. You're immature [...] I lost my virginity when I was 14-years-old!" Dale: "Really?"

But since Franco didn't write or direct *Pineapple Express*, we'll ignore that film and, in addition to Herbert White (2010), take a look at Franco's *Bukowski* (2013), *High School Lover* (2017), and *Mother, May I Sleep with Danger?* (2016).

Franco directed and co-wrote *Bukowski* (2013), but despite settling a lawsuit over film rights, the film was never released. Per the *Hollywood Reporter*: "In media interviews, Franco has expressed fondness for *Ham on Rye* [Charles Bukowski's novel].

Because Franco directed and co-wrote *Bukowski,* we can safely take a stretch and infer that Franco's a Bukowski fan, we can deduce that Franco has devoured more than *Ham on Rye,* and we wouldn't be blamed for presuming that Bukowski has influenced Franco's prose and poems.

As for Bukowski, he wrote about driving down Wilton Avenue in the poem "Sex":

> when this girl of about 15
>
> dressed in tight blue jeans
>
> that grip her behind like two hands
>
> steps out in front of my car
>
> I stop to let her cross the street
>
> and as I watch her contours waving
>
> she looks directly through my windshield
>
> at me.

"In a clean, well-lighted place" Bukowski wrote in reference to Ernest Hemingway:

> the old fart. he used his literary reputation
>
> to reel them in one at a time,

each younger than the last.
he liked to meet them for luncheon and
wine
and he'd talk and listen to them
talk.
whatever wife or girlfriend he had at the moment
was made to
understand that this sort of thing made him
"young again."
the young ladies vied to bed down with
this
literary
genius.
In between, he continued to write,
and late at night in his favorite bar
he liked to talk about writing and his amorous
adventures.
actually, he was just a drunk
who liked young ladies,
writing itself,
and talking about writing.
wasn't a bad life.

And in "man mowing the lawn across the way from me" Bukowski
wrote:

man mowing the lawn across from me
don't you see the young girls walking down the sidewalks
now

with knives in their purses?
don't you see their beautiful eyes and dresses and
hair?
don't you see their beautiful asses and knees and
ankles?"

While Franco's *Bukowski* wasn't released, a number of other films and documentaries have been released that are based on and about Bukowski's life. For example, in the opening scene of *Tales of Ordinary Madness* (1981) [Italian: Storie di ordinaria follia], after being applauded for a poetry reading, Bukowski (Ben Gazzara) literally stumbled upon a blond nymphet in a satin laced sky blue dress in the theater's auditorium. The blond passionately kissed Charles on the lips before she revealed that she was 12-years-old and pleaded with him to let her accompany him to Hollywood. After Bukowski messaged her chest, he questioned her age due to size of her fountains. Caught in a bold face lie, she admitted that she was 14-years-old. Subsequently, Charles awoke up from a drunken stupor with his slacks unzipped and discovered that the nymphet had vanished along with his Greyhound bus ticket. However, she left him a pair of white panties inscribed with the message "Love You".

In the very last scene of the film, which won the Silver Ribbon from the Italian National Syndicate of Film Journalists, Bukowski, once again in a drunken stupor, literally stumbled upon a nymphet (sixteen-year-old Katya Berger). She was a pony tailed brunette in a pink top, blue jeans and Nike sneakers. She stopped feeding sea gulls to gaze upon Bukowski who had collapsed on the beach. "Will you write me a poem?" the nymphet asked Bukowski. "What will you give me for it?" Bukowski replied before he rubbed her left nipple through her top. "You show me your titties and I will compose a poem. Just for you." Subsequently, Bukowski read "The Sun Wields Mercy" as the nymphet removed her clothes and caressed the poet's hands as he caressed her young and firm fountains.

Tales of Ordinary Madness (1981) was based on Bukowski's collection of short stories *Erections, Ejaculations, Exhibitions* and *General Tales of Ordinary Madness*. Those books were subsequently republished into two volumes: *Tales of Ordinary Madness* and *The Most Beautiful Woman in Town* and were littered with nympholepsy. For example, in the short story "The White Beard", the protagonist, who worked as a fruit picker in Mexico, was approached by a "young girl of 13 or 14, origin unknown [...] Her eyes were milky blue [...] and the poor child was nothing but breasts." The Mexican teen prostitute inquired, "They make you hot, don't they? You want to fuck me?" As the protagonist sucked on the nymphet's breasts "a tear came down! It was so good, a tear did come down. A tear of placid joy." But he was admonished by his colleagues, because he didn't "fuck the breasts". Subsequently, Herb, the protagonist's colleague, "rammed it between her breasts. Then a sea of come [formed] under her chin. When she stood up it hung there like a white beard. She needed two towels to mop it up."

While Franco only starred in *Pineapple Express*, not only did he star in *High School Lover* (2017), he executive produced the Lifetime film as well. Here's the Movie Info from Rotten

Tomatoes: A [17-years-old] teenage girl starts dating an older [26-years-old] famous actor, much to her father's [James Franco] dismay, but their romance puts her family in danger when her beau's adoration spirals into obsession."

Interestingly, *High School Lover* was written by two women - Jessica Dube and Amber Viera. And here's a taste of the dialogue that took place between two high school coeds four minutes into the film:

> "I hope you're not wearing that dress your dad got you."
> "Screw you bitch!"
> "Yes! Please! You know at least someone would be getting screwed here."

In the film, Kelley Winters (Paulina Singer), the 17-year-old high school student, met Christian Booth, the 26-year-old famous actor, at an exclusive party. While Kelly's high school mates snorted cocaine, Christian asked Kelly, "How old are you?" But before Kelly could answer, Christian said, "Actually, don't tell me."

After they left the party, one of Kelly's classmates demanded, "You have to have sex with him (i.e., Christian Booth); so, I'll know what it's like." Subsequently, Kelly's classmate inquired, "Did you get the D?"

Later, after Christian introduced himself to Kelly's dad, Kelly's dad informed, "You know they're all seventeen - right? How old are you?" Christian responded, "Twenty-six sir." [Note: Since the age-of-consent in New York, where the film was filmed and set, is 17, the film doesn't follow the spirit of the law or the letter.

Otherwise, Kelly's dad would have been content that she was 17 (i.e., of legal age).]

Against her father's wishes, Kelly continued her affair with Christian, and after the age-gap couple took a helicopter ride, where Kelly performed oral sex on Christian, Christian antagonistically sexted the video to Kelly's father.

I won't spoil the ending of the teen romance slash thriller, but I will share a revealing conversation:

Christian, "She was begging [for sex], alright."
Kelly's dad, "She's seventeen!"
Christian, "Yeah. Yeah. I know. That's why is was so good."

Interestingly, Jerell Rosales, the film's director, made it a point of displaying Kelly in her bra and panties, Kelly's dad [Franco] was ten years older than Kelly's step-mother, and Paulina Singer [Kelly] played Madison in *The Nymphets* (2015), which per IMDb is about: "A precarious man [who] invites a group of wild young girls to his loft to party even though he knows it's a terrible idea."

The Lifetime film poster for *Mother, May I Sleep with Danger?* (2016) reads "From the twisted mind of James Franco". And we culled from Rotten Tomatoes that Rabbit Bandini Productions, which was co-founded by Franco, was one of the production companies for the film, Franco co-executive produced the film, and Franco wrote the story that the script was based upon.

Interestingly, Franco's story was based upon *Mother, May I Sleep with Danger?* (1996). In a 2016 interview with *Entertainment Tonight*, Franco spoke about the differences between the 1996 and 2016 versions of the films, "I wanted to change things a little bit." That was an understatement, because the 1996 version of the film had no coed lipstick lesbians.

Even though most of the film is set on a college campus, the opening scene may be the most relevant. In the scene, Pearl's (Emily Meade) lipstick lesbian girlfriend suggested that they go upstairs, "My parents are out.". After asking her girlfriend to photograph her in seductive poses, "I'll be your muse," the two girls kissed *sur son lit*. Subsequently, Pearl's girlfriend informed Pearl, "I'm a nightwalker [...] It's like a vampire." Interestingly, the subsequent scene took place "Five Years Later", when Leah is an undergraduate theater major, which would make Leah, at the minimum, a first semester high school senior (i.e., 17-years-old) when the first scene was set. Thus, we'll infer that Pearl was in high school as well with further evidence being that instead of making out, Pearl and her vampire girlfriend had planned to see *The Twilight Saga: New Moon* (2009) - a teen film.

In the next scene, Leah is attending a lecture on Vampires & Sexuality where she gives an analysis of the *Twilight* series of books:

"The first Twilight book was good, because it made teen sex dangerous again [...] In the past, teen sex was forbidden. A pregnancy out of wedlock was like death. But now, in our day, we have *Teen Mom* shows and everyone can just use condoms. The first *Twilight* book was great, because it equated teen sex with death again. And then they screwed it up in the later books when he starts holding out because he's a "Victorian gentleman." And then they actually get married as teens to have sex, which is just a way to cash in on teen sexuality while trying to seem morally responsible. It's absurd."

Stephenie Meyer is one of the most successful female novelists of all time. Meyer's *Twilight* series of books have sold over one hundred million copies, were translated into over thirty-five languages, and were successfully adapted to the big screen – earning Stephanie over $50 million dollars; however, did you know that *Twilight*, which was a *New York Times* Editor's Choice, an Amazon "Best Book of the Decade" and a *Publishers Weekly* Best Book of the Year, is based on an age-discrepant relationship? What I did not realize, despite all the hoopla surrounding the books and movies, was that Edward, who was played by the heartthrob Robert Pattinson, was close to ninety-years-old. In the novel, high school student Bella (Kristen Stewart) asked Edward, "How old are you?"

"Seventeen," he answered promptly.

"And how long have you been seventeen?"

"A while," he admitted at last.

Interestingly, the way Bella asked the questions and the way she reacted to Edward's answers were markedly different in the book than in the movie. In the book, the tone of Bella's questions was relaxed, and she appeared to be relieved and even pleased with

Edward's answers. However, in the movie, Bella was extremely tense and distraught, both in her questions and her reaction to Edward's responses. In the book, Bella smiled when she found out the Edward had been seventeen for "awhile," but in the movie, she looked like she had just found out that her entire family had been killed in a JFK bound airplane crash.

It turned out that Edward's vague answer did not satisfy the 17-year-old Bella's curiosity. She pressed on, and maintained a soft tone, this time in the book and the film, for a more specific answer.

> "Are you ever going to tell me how old you are?" I asked, tentative, not wanting to upset his buoyant humor.
> "Does it matter much?" His smile, to my relief, remained unclouded.
> "No, but I still wonder […]" I grimaced. "There's nothing like an unsolved mystery to keep you up at night."
> "I wonder if it will upset you," he reflected to himself.
> "Try me," I finally said.
> "I was born in Chicago in 1901."

Bella feigned an unsurprised look on her face and braced herself for more information about the much older man she was, as the back cover of the book describes, "unconditionally, and irrevocably in love with".

My initial response to Edward's birthdate was shock, but then I passed it off as a sub-plot that was probably missed by most of the fans of the series. That was until I took an unscientific poll from a variety of teenage fans of the series. I asked a number of nymphets if they were aware of Edward's age and every single one of them replied in the affirmative; however, the knowledge of Edward's age did not sway their opinion of the books or the movies in any way.

With that, let's conclude this chapter, but as you can see, Franco's oeuvre is liberally peppered with nympholepsy, which raises the question: "Is James Franco a (open) nympholept?" Let's take a look at Franco's Instagram scandal, which may shed some light on the answer.

Chapter 2

The Instagram Scandal

Per Ridley's *The Red Queen,* that *New York Times* Notable Book we mentioned previously, research shows that (heteronormative) men are attracted to a trinity of qualities: youth, figure, and face. And like we mentioned previously, *men are inherently nympholepts*, but, due to low levels of self-confidence and self-esteem, most men don't initiate age-gap relationships with nymphets, and in what may be counterintuitive to teen boys and middle-aged women, on the contrary, most age-gap relationships involving teens are, whether in fiction or nonfiction, initiated by nymphets.

For example, if we revisit Elvis, Suzanne Finstad related in *Child Bride: The Untold Story of Priscilla Beaulieu Presley* that 14-year-old Priscilla had sex with Curry Grant, a 27-seven-year-old friend of Elvis, in exchange for being introduced to Elvis. And remember Porter and Prince wrote that Elizabeth Taylor disclosed: "[36-year-old future president Ronald] Reagan was treating me like a grown woman, and that thrilled me. We sat on his sofa and I could tell he wanted to get it on, but he seemed reluctant [because I was 15-years-old] to make the first move [so] I became the aggressor."

And you may know that Anthony Weiner was sentenced to 21 months in prison for sexting with a 15-year-old high school sophomore. But did you know that the nymphet initiated the relationship? Alana Goodman related some inside information from the teen in a somewhat misleadingly titled *Daily Mail* piece "Anthony Weiner carried on a months-long online sexual relationship with a troubled 15-year-old girl telling her she made him 'hard,' asking her to dress up in 'school-girl' outfits and pressing her to engage in 'rape fantasies'". Goodman wrote:

> [...] the girl said she did not want to press charges because she believes her relationship with Weiner was consensual.

> The girl first reached out to Weiner on the evening of January 23, 2016, when she noticed his Twitter page allowed non-followers to contact him through direct private messages.

> She told DailyMail.com she was interested in politics and had heard about his sexting scandals and was curious to see what he was like.

> It was clear from the messages that she was encouraging Weiner to engage with her in a sexual manner.

> She told DailyMail.com she didn't consider Weiner her boyfriend, but thought the relationship was a 'romantic' one.

> She acknowledged during interviews that she had developed an obsession with Weiner and sought him out on Twitter in January while trying to write a book about

him. She said she continued to write the book as their relationship developed.

In addition to *Lolita*, there are hundreds of examples in fiction of teens seducing men. For example, in the French film *Beau-père* (1981) after her mother died, 14-year-old Marion fell in love with Rémi - her stepfather. Rémi: "I'm too old for little girls." Marion: "I'm not a little girl anymore. I'm a [young] woman." However, Rémi eventually succumbed to Marion's seductive advances and began an affair with the nymphet.

In Anne Rice's *Belinda*, 44-year-old Jeremy Walker, a famous author and artist, was seduced by Belinda - a blond and tanned 16-year-old. The affair began after Belinda wantonly attended Walker's book signing. Upon seeing Belinda, Walker imagined, "Reaching under her short little Catholic school plaid skirt and touching the silk of her naked thighs [...] kissing her, seeing if her face was as soft as it looked-baby flesh."

And Sarah DeLappe's *The Wolves*, among other accolades, was a finalist for the 2017 Pulitzer Prize for Drama and a 2016 *New York Times* Critic's Pick. The play was originally produced at The Duke on 42nd Street before it moved to the Lincoln Center. Here's part of Wikipedia's synopsis: ""The Wolves" is set in an indoor soccer facility. Each scene depicts the nine teenage girls that make up the Wolves, a soccer team, warming up before their game each week." In the play, in reference to Coach Mikhail, who played professional soccer in Croatia or Czech Republic, #14 opined: I think he's sorta sexy. #8 exclaimed: he's like 45!! But #14 retorted: so's Jude Law.

If we accept that men are inherently nympholepts and that (most) age-gap affairs involving nymphets are, in fact, initiated by nymphets, then it should come as no surprise that teens and young women left the following comments on Franco's Instagram:

> kristinevalentine22: I wanna bang you so bad james
>
> serentaiii: FUCK me
>
> garasalas: Someday i'll rape u
>
> sabrina_jasmine: Fuckkkk me
>
> nicoledoriano: Fuck me
>
> giovannabasilio: How young is too young?

And only God and Franco knows about the salacious direct messages (DMs) Franco received. However, Franco gave us a hint about the contents of his DMs when he posted on his Instagram account: (PLEASE DON'T DM IF YOU ARE UNDER 18. THANK YOU)

In addition, it should come as no surprise that Franco DMed a nymphet(s). It would be (almost) inhuman for Franco to be able to remain passive after having read such salacious comments. However, it's often the case that when an age-gap affair between a man and a teen is revealed to the public, the man is trolled, and the nymphet is consoled. And that is exactly what happened to Franco.

Per a *Dlisted* post, "James Franco Tried To Pick Up A 17-Year-Old On Instagram", Franco invited Lucy Clode, a Scottish teen, to a hotel *rendez-vous* after he signed her autograph and took a selfie with her outside of the Longacre Theatre where he starred in

Of Mice and Men. Clode tagged Franco when she posted the selfie on Instagram, which allowed Franco to DM the blonde nymphet.

Wait, remember The Villain from *Actors Anonymous?* Well, he revealed his technique for procuring nymphets: "One of my favorite approaches was to ask the young girls that requested to take a photo with me to email me a copy of the photo; that way I can give them my info very quickly in front of a crowd of fans and later work out a way to see them." Sound familiar?

Anyway, per screenshots, here's the Instagram DM conversation that took place between jamesfrancotv (i.e., James Franco) and lucy_clode:

Jamesfrancotv: Hi

lucy_clode: Hi [scared cat emoji]

jamesfrancotv: Where do you live?

Jamesfrancotv: NYC?

lucy_clode: Scotland

lucy_clode: In a small town called Dollar

jamesfrancotv: How long will you be in New York?

lucy_clode: Oops sorry, um a few days it's my 18th birthday present

jamesfrancotv: You're 18?

Jamesfrancotv: Who are you with?

lucy_clode: Nearly 18, my mum and not if you're around [Three (3) smiling face with heart-eyes emojis]

jamesfrancotv: When is your bday?

Jamesfrancotv: Where are you staying?

Jamesfrancotv: What's your #?

<u>lucy_clode:</u> In May but I have exams then, just off of Times Square in a Hilton, what do you mean #?

Subsequently, the conversation moved to iMessage:

<u>Franco:</u> Can I see you?

<u>Clode:</u> As long as you are james Franco

<u>Franco:</u> I am\You're single?\What's the hotel?\Should I rent a room?

<u>Clode:</u> April fools was an hour ago though…

<u>Franco:</u> (Franco sent a selfie.)\It's me\Yes or no?\Tomorrow or thurs?\Ok\Be wll\X

<u>Clode:</u> I'll come back when I'm 18

<u>Franco:</u> X

<u>Clode:</u> Well this is a story my Scotish friends will never believe

<u>Franco:</u> Don't tell

<u>Clode:</u> I just want proper evidence that it's you and I won't

<u>Franco:</u> I gave it to you\If you don't want to meet, then text me\When you do\Bye

<u>Clode:</u> You sound so dodgy though

<u>Franco:</u> Bye

<u>Clode:</u> One second, I will meet you if you write my name on a piece of paper then send it to me your face also in the picture. please

<u>Franco:</u> [Franco sent a selfie with Clode's first name written in capital letters.]

As you can cull from the DMs and iMessages, there were two sources of contention between Franco and Clode. 1. Clode wanted to verify Franco's identity. 2. Initially, despite the fact that the age-of-consent in New York is 17 and it's 16 in Scotland, Clode didn't want to meet Franco until after her 18th birthday. However, Clode decided that if she could unequivocally verify Franco's identity, she would meet him at a hotel.

Interestingly, Lauren Duca and Ryan Kristobak wrote the *Huffington Post* piece "So, Is James Franco's Use Of Instagram Innovative Film Promotion Or Just Kind Of Creepy?" and implied that the Franco\Clode scandal may have been a publicity stunt to promote Franco's *Palo Alto* (2013).

Franco discussed the Instagram scandal on *The Howard Stern Show*:

> "They (i.e., the media) make it out like I'm pursuing young women (i.e., teens). I'm not going to high schools - you know looking for dates. I'm leaving my work, and they're coming there! [...] So, I'm just, I'm seeing attractive [young] women. And look, my fan base is like, you know, 17-year-old girls. Like if I do a book signing, it'll be 17-year-old to, you know, 30-year-old women. That's my, that's my biggest fan base. So, they're out there - outside the theater every night. You come down to, you know, 48th street, that's what you're gonna see at, you know, 10:30. (Stern: So, who can blame you for that?") So, I saw her and umm (Stern: She was hot?) she's saying on her page: "I *love* James Franco blah, blah, blah, blah, blah."

OK. (Stern: Great!) Well, I, you look interesting. I don't know how old you are. Uh, I was, you know, a gentleman. I said, "Ah, do you have a boyfriend?" And her response was, "Not when you're around." (Stern: Laughs.) So that to me sounds like, "OK, she's interested." (Stern: Right.) [...]

Franco shared that he didn't believe that Clode posted the DMs and iMessages to defame him and before the segment ended, Franco went on to relate:

> "And here's the other thing. Like, I'm not gonna call out any names but like [...] dude every celebrity does it! Men and women. I've seen - I've been on so many movies where this, you know, happens [...] Everybody does it! Oscar winners that I know. [...] I just was reading Dennis Hoppers - a biography of Dennis Hopper and he talks about going to meet Elvis. "Yeah, there were like six women outside his hotel room just lined up and they'd go in one-by-one." Like, oh my God!" (Stern: How old was Priscilla when he met her? 14 right? There you go.) Look. Let's not get into ages. For me, it's not about. I did not, when I met her. It was about how she looked not about, "Oh, you're young? Let me fucking meet you! Like, that was not what was going on."

However, I think that we can confidently assume that if Clode were one of Franco's 30-year-old fans, he would *not* have DMed her, which reminds me of the famous writer Leslie Goodwin (John Malkovich) in Louis C.K.'s *I Love You, Daddy (2017)* who confessed to 17-year-old China (Chloë Grace Moretz) that he frequently went to Barneys to gawk at Manhattan's elite schoolgirls.

China: "You like looking at young girls?"
Leslie: "Sure, who doesn't. I mean if you had a choice between looking at a pretty girl your age or a retired bus driver, who would you choose?"

Franco revealed on *Live with Kelly & Michael* that he was feeling awkward, embarrassed, like a model of how social media is tricky, and that he used bad judgement, but that he learned his lesson.

Consequently, the Franco\Clode scandal, to the dismay of nymphets all over the world, led to Franco's departure from social media. But before he left, he posted a meme that was created by a detractor. In the meme, Franco is wearing a pair of sunglasses and dressed in a scarf (cashmere?) and a black overcoat with the caption: "WHY ARE YOU THIRSTY FOR UNDERAGE ONES" To which Franco replied: "I'M NOT! I HOPE PARENTS KEEP THEIR TEENS AWAY FROM ME. Thank you"

Würger elaborated in her *New York Times* book review:

There is a type of entertainment [e.g., *Law & Order: SVU*] that wants to have it both ways: to feed off its audience's lurid interest in rape and murder and torture, but also to present itself as performing a socially important function, as if it were an earnest and necessary exposé about the unfortunate prevalence of rape and murder and torture.

And what are some of the gruesome subject matters that *Law & Order: SVU* allows viewers to partake in without feeling dirty? Well, there's the 16th season premiere that was about teen prostitutes. Fans of the drama were introduced to the first "underage prostitute" as she was about to perform oral sex on a middle-aged john in a SUV - in broad daylight. Subsequently, a house with four additional teen prostitutes, one white and two Latina, was raided. Episode 5 of season 16 was inspired by Anthony Weiner's sexting scandal, which may have caused him to lose the New York City mayoral candidate primary race. However, the difference between Weiner and Alex Munoz, *Law & Order: SVU's* mayoral candidate, is that Munoz solicited and exchanged pictures on the website PleasureWithoutConscience.com with Jodie, a 15-year-old Grant high school student, which put the candidate: "[...] in possession of child pornography." And episode 17 of Season 18 was about a teen prostitution ring that was organized by the Catholic Church, which provided nymphets for hire to New York City elected officials.

Thus, it should come as no surprise that there's an episode of *Law & Order: SVU* that's based on the Franco\Clode Instagram scandal. Franco's *Law & Order: SVU* episode was subtitled Agent Provocateur. Here's IMDb's plot summary season 16 episode 11 - Agent Provocateur:

An actor is suspected of raping a 15-year-old girl, but are he and his agent trying to spin it into a publicity stunt for his new movie? And why is a tabloid journalist keeping the NYPD from discovering the truth?

Per usual, the episode began with the disclaimer: The following story is fictional and does not depict any actual person or event. After getting the legalities out of the way, Madison, the 15-year-old, departed an Upper West Side doorman building and hopped into a yellow cab before she removed her overcoat to reveal a revealing black dress. The nymphet uncapped a bottle of gin and happily glossed her lips.

In the next scene, she was zipped into a suitcase, dragged through Tribeca's Howell hotel's lobby and left for dead in an alley with gin, Ambien, Xanax and condom lubricant in her system. Utilizing a racist trope, Madison told Sergeant Benson and Detective Amaro, two of NYPD's finest, that before she could meet with a "friend" to see *Wicked,* she was drugged by a "Middle Eastern maybe" cab driver.

NYPD discovered, via an Instagram post, that Madison's "friend" was Scott Russo (Shiloh Fernandez) whom was described as a "[pretty boy] actor slash painter slash philosopher" and a "Renaissance man". Sound familiar? It was revealed that Madison was obsessed with Russo, she watched Russo's *Caspien Sea* (N.D.) - ten times, and that the age-gap couple met via Twitter DMs. Sound familiar?

After being questioned about his relationship with Madison, Russo shared with Ice T's character, "After *Caspian Sea,* that's my fan base, young girls. There's a bunch of them in the lobby right now. Some of them always manage to slip under the [proverbial] velvet rope" Sound familiar?

In a scene right out of Franco's Instagram scandal, Russo took a break from promoting *Falsely Accused*, to take a selfie with his screaming teen fans. "Y'all just went up on Instagram." And the episode implied that the Madison and Russo scandal was a publicity stunt for Russo's film. But after a waiter told the NYPD that Russo was seen doing "body shots" off of Madison's nubile body, Russo confessed, "Alright look. I invited her to the party. We had some drinks. I find out that she was underage; so, I excused myself. She followed me to my room. Alright, if you would have watched the playback on that [LMZ] video, you would have seen that I shut the door on her."

Madison confirmed Russo's claim and proclaimed to her mother in front of NYPD, "I am not a child! And he [Russo] didn't attack me. I followed him to his room! I wanted to be with him [...] He didn't force me. We're soul mates. I've been dreaming that this would happen. That he would fall in love with me."

Madison went on to disclose with her mother and the NYPD that after Russo told her that she was a nice girl but that she was too young for him, she went to Skye Adderson's room, Russo's co-star, and had sex with him and that she lied initially because, "I didn't want Scott [Russo] to find out that I had cheated on him. I knew that he would never forgive me."

Ultimately, the motion to dismiss the indictment against Russo was "so ordered", and he left the courthouse to the cheers of Madison and a gaggle of additional nymphets. Sadly, even though Madison confessed to the NYPD that <u>she</u> aggressively attempted to have sex with Russo and that it was <u>her</u> idea to go to Adderson's hotel room for sex, she didn't receive even a slap on her *jeune* wrist. Why? Because it's inconceivable to many that a nymphet would desire to have consensual sex with an older man.

Chapter 3

The Daddy Thing

Here are some of the "daddy thing" comments left on Franco's Instagram account:

kimyakiarash: daddy

6.17am: Daddy

slurpee.girrl: Omg hi papi

kimyakiarash: I love you daddy ;)

amberosinski: dad

_itsshainee: Hi daddy

yarisssa: Zaddy

urlilbaby: DADDY

amberosinski: hi dad

amberosinski: …..dad?

yamiibear: Let me call you daddy (:

jessikamancillas: BABY DADDY SO DAM FINE.

slurpee.girrl: Babe I am legal, u can fuck me n not get in trouble 4 it papi

As shocking as these comments may be to some, in popular culture the "daddy thing" is actually quite "normal". Remember Lana Del Ray's "Little Girls (Put Me In A Movie)": "Come on, you know you like little girls\You can be my daddy"?

Another example is when I did a Google search for a video of Angelina Jolie in *Cyborg 2* (1993) that resulted in a post on *The Allure of Nymphets* blog titled "CYBORG 2: Nude Teen Angelina Jolie in Age-Gap Sex Scene" where a topless 17-year-old Jolie performed in a sex scene with 31-year-old Elias Koteas.

The Google search sent me to Pornhub where I consequently came across a video starring a stunningly beautiful 18-year-old teen whom seductively said the following into the camera:

Thank you daddy for tucking me in tonight. I know I'm older now, and I haven't asked you to do this in a long time. It just kind of reminded me of when I was little and we were closer. Don't you miss those times? Well, there's something I actually wanted to talk to you about tonight. Umm, now that I'm getting older, I am experiencing some changes in my body - in my mood. Have you noticed anything different about me daddy? (After she pulls down the left strap of her Mickey Mouse t-shirt to reveal even more cleavage.) Do you like the way I look Daddy? Well, even though I'm older now, there is [*sic*] still things I need from you. I need attention [...] It's a little embarrassing, but I'm still a virgin. And I've been waiting for the right guy. And, I don't know, you've always been there for me. You taught me how to ride my first bike; so, why not teach me how to ride my first cock. Oh come on daddy, I won't tell. Mom would never know. And it would just be our little secret. We both know that I've always kinda been a daddy's girl [...] And I just want you to show me how to take real cock like a good little girl.

Maureen O'Connor related in her *New York* magazine cover story "Pornhub is the Kinsey Report of Our Time" that, per data culled from Pornhub: "[...] women were 96% more likely than men to use dad-related search terms [e.g., "dad" and "daddy"]".

After a day of tutoring teens, I used to drop off into the American Apparel on 8th avenue for the latest issue of *Vice* magazine. In one such issue was Brett Gelman's short story *Santa Daddy* where Angela invited a middle-aged bearded man to her apartment. After she asked him to put on a Santa Claus costume, they had the following conversation:

> Angela: "Spank me, Santa Daddy! Spank that ass, Santa Daddy! Spank that 16-year-old ass! Merry Christmas!"
> Santa Daddy: "Sixteen? I thought you said you were 20!"
> Angela: "Did I? Oops! Guess I'm even less nice than you thought!"

Unsurprisingly, the short story was accompanied by a photograph of Gelman, in a Santa costume, spanking Angela's bare rear end.

Here's part of Amazon's plot summary for Megan Abbott's coming-of-age novel *The End of Everything*:

> Thirteen-year old Lizzie Hood and her next door neighbor Evie Verver are inseparable [...] And then, one afternoon, Evie disappears [...] Would she have gotten into the car of

a stranger? [...] Lizzie uncovers secrets and lies that make her wonder if she knew her best friend at all.

However, the reviewer failed to mention that Lizzie was in love with her best friend's father: "Oh, and Mr. Verver, Mr. Verver, Mr. Verver, he's always vibrating in my chest, under my fingernails, in all kinds of places [...] I couldn't remember a time when I wasn't [...] hungry for the moments he would shine his attentions on me."

The Amazon review mentioned that Evie disappeared but understandably didn't reveal that Evie voluntarily disappeared for three weeks with Mr. Shaw: "Evie felt Mr. Shaw's love [...] a man three times her age [...] and knows that she is the most special girl of all [...] She is everything and he would tear down his life for her [...] She has that power. What girl wouldn't want that power?" Evie confessed to Lizzie, "I went with him. I wanted to go. I asked him to take me away."

Now here's the part of *The End of Everything* that's most relevant to this chapter. Dusty, Evie's sister and a high school coed, called her sister "a disgusting little girl" for having a sexual affair with Mr. Shaw, but Evie retorted by revealing Dusty's incestuous flirting with their father: "And you stand her blaming me, judging me, but look at you, Dusty, preening for him [...] the flirting and the winking and the curling up to him in our lawn chairs, I see how it is, Mom sees how it is. I know what you feel. You think you can hide it, but you can't. Who's the sick one, who is --"

Interestingly, *The End of Everything* is in the Highbrow/Brilliant quadrant of *New York* magazine's Approval Matrix (June 27, 2011).

In *Solitary Man* (2009), Ben Kalmen (Michael Douglas) took Allyson (Imogen Poots), his step-daughter and a senior in high school, to visit his alma mater in Boston. During the night of the college tour, Ben and his step-daughter had sex in the hotel, but back in Manhattan, Ben became "clingy" to which Allyson responded by saying:

> "Come on Ben [...] I thought there was going to be a little difference between you and the guys my age. You wouldn't go simple and be all clingy and stuff [...] It was a kick. It was really, really fun. But now I can check two things off my list. Despite the end of [the] Daddy thing." To which Ben inquired, "The Daddy thing?"

In 2014, I went to see *Intimacy*, a play, at the Acorn Theater on west 42nd street. Before I entered the theater, a sign warned: "Please Note: This show contains nudity, sex and bad language. Enjoy!" But I had been forewarned by New York City Theater's website, which posted that *Intimacy* was a: "[...] "boisterous and revealing dark comedy about race, sex and intimacy."

In the play, which was written by Thomas Bradshaw, a professor of playwriting at Northwestern University, James (Daniel Gerrol) informed his neighbor Jerry (Keith Smith) that Jerry's 18-year-old daughter, Janet (Ella Dershowitz), had nude pictures in the latest issue of *Barely Legal* magazine. Consequently, James accused Jerry of being a bad parent. Initially, James <u>and</u> Jerry were understandably distraught.

In a subsequent scene, to console her father, Janet told him that she loves sex and that she had her first orgasm when she was 13 while watching porn on his computer. Shockingly, Janet encouraged her father to masturbate to her nude photograph and "cum" on her face.

Nancy Friday's revealing *My Secret Garden: Women's Sexual Fantasies* is an international bestselling collection of women's fantasies that were collected during the early 1970s via interviews and letters from women from a variety of races and socioeconomic classes. Most of the women who contributed to the book shared that they started fantasizing when they were nymphets - more specifically, most of the women began fantasizing when they were between the ages of 7 and 11.

A number of women shared with Friday that they had fantasies about bestiality (e.g., more than several of the women fantasized about their dogs performing oral sex on them.), being raped (often by more than one man), sex with multiple men and\or women "alone" or in front of audiences, sex with African-American men were common fantasies, and most relevantly, some women confessed that their fantasies involved incest. Furthermore, I was surprised to learn that, ironically, (some) lesbians picture men while having lesbian sex. However, I wasn't surprised to learn that some women enjoy glancing at "crotches", because I've eyed nubile nymphets on the Uptown 4 snapping pics of men's crotches. Here are some of the fantasies:

1. Clarissa related that she remembers when she and her friend were caught masturbating with candles when they were 12.

2. Marina began to be aware of men at the age of 9 or 10 and thought about them while she masturbated; however, Marina only had "a vague idea of what lovemaking was" until she met her friend - a 10-year-old Mediterranean girl. Marina and the Mediterranean nymphet used to sit at opposite ends of the bathtub and pour warm water from a Russian silver teapot all over their clitorises while caressing their bodies "with infallible, instinctive verve."

3. Theda's first sexual fantasy started after she gazed upon her teacher's "rotund posterior" when she was about 7 or 8. She wrote that she had "an infantile urge" to slide her hand "…down his bum cheeks and round to 'the front'…". And when she was 14, her friend Monica "…allowed boys to feel her while she undid their flies and 'tossed them off'.

4. Alexandra had fantasies about having an affair with her high school teacher. She stated emphatically, "…I'm sure it would not be a fantasy if I gave him a little encouragement." I concur.

5. And Bella revealed that since she was 8-years-old, her father has always been her "fantasy lover during masturbation".

Some men use this daddy fetish to their advantage. For example, the former founder and CEO of American Apparel referred to himself as Dov "Daddy" Charney.

Sapna Maheshwari reported in the Buzzfeed article "American Apparel Reveals X-Rated Alleged Messages Between Founder And Staff" that American Apparel (AA) leaked explicit text messages and emails between teen staff members and Dov Charney. The revelations were in response to a May 2015 defamation lawsuit filed by Charney. Some examples are: "Jack off fun for a bad daddy." and "Daddy is so excited to play with the most little tiny blonde cum kitten in the whole school."

In 2011, Charney was sued by Irene Morales who claimed that 38-year-old Charney began seducing her when she was 17 and on her 18th birthday he had anal sex with her before styling her as his sex slave. However, Charney purported that Morales voluntarily sent him revealing text messages and emails - some of which were posted by Gawker. In one text, Irene shared with Dov "Daddy" Charney: "I bought a fat dildo...." and in an email to Daddy, the teen wrote: "Oh pwease [*sic*] ....send me my wittle birthday wishlist....do it for all those delicious blowjobs I would give you, and how I would lick your little asshoel clean!!! And how I would love to do it again when I see you!!!!"

On episode eleven of the first season of Showtime's *Shameless*, Karen, a high school sophomore, attended a Purity Ball with her father with the idea that Karen would vow to re-purify and remain pure until she got married. As part of the ceremony, the nymphets were asked to share their previous impure activities in front of their fathers. Patty shared that she let a choir boy touch her breasts through her shirt and bra and that she felt his "rod" touch her leg. After Patty was thanked for her courage to confront her struggles with desire, Karen, in a pure white dress, disclosed the following:

> "I started having oral sex at a very young age, maybe 13, with guys around the neighborhood. Three of four at first. Then well, more than three or four. I didn't have intercourse until the 8th grade. I didn't like it at first, but then around the 6th time it started to feel good - really good. But I didn't feel good about it. Umm, there was [*sic*] a few times where I got high and started experimenting with guys and girls - at the same time. I wouldn't necessarily call it an orgy, but there were a lot of naked body parts flying around, which felt very good, but kinda bad all at the same time. And then there was the time at Mindy Karlson's sleepover when we all got in the shower and started soaping each other up. Then her mom walked in and freaked out when she saw Mindy in the shower with a big black strap-on dildo. To which Karen's father interjected: "You whore!""

Consequently, Karen, distraught after her father called her a whore in front of the other Purity Ball attendees, decided to get revenge by creating Daddyz Girl - an online diary. On the website, Karen live streamed herself having sex with her mother's married boyfriend (i.e., step-father?).

Here's Wikipedia's plot summary for the Netflix's *Insatiable* (2018):

Patty Bladell is a teenager who was constantly bullied in school for being overweight. After being on a liquid diet for three months over summer vacation because of a freak accident, she is now thin and seeks revenge on her bullies. A disgraced civil lawyer and obsessed beauty pageant coach, Bob Armstrong, notices Patty's potential and sets out to turn her into a pageant queen.

I read a number of plot summaries for the dark comedy, but none of them mentioned that 17-year-old Patty attempted to seduce Bob. Bob didn't even know. Bob said, "I had no idea she wanted to seduce me." *Insatiable* was surrounded by controversy due to 'fat-shaming', but no one seemed to voice any opposition to Patty's attraction to her pageant coach. For instance, Patty opined, referring to Bob, "He's a man and a total DILF (i.e., Dad I'd Love [to] Fuck)." When Patty was told that Bob was (falsely) accused of being a child molester, she replied, "Which means I might actually have a shot!" Patty justified her attempt to seduce Bob by stating, "Cleopatra had seduced some much older man, but I preferred a more contemporary role model. Drew Barrymore as Amy Fisher (i.e., the Long Island Lolita) - the greatest seductress in American history. " Patty planned, "In a couple of months I'd be 18, and then Bob's resting anus face wife would be the only thing left standing in my way." And Patty asked Bob, "Can I call you Daddy?"

Way before *Insatiable* started streaming on Netflix, FX ran *Nip/Tuck,* which Google described as:

[...] campy series [that] centers on the office of Dr. Sean McNamara [Dylan Walsh] and Dr. Christian Troy, longtime friends who practice surgery (and live life) in two entirely different ways. Christian is the stereotypical self-destructive playboy. Sean is the family man facing a moral crossroads, as well as a failed marriage to Julia.

On episode 7 of season 5, after Eden (AnnaLynne McCord), an 18-year-old high school student, had "get it out of our system" sex with Dr. McNamara, she decided to abruptly leave the plastic surgeon's apartment and go "out" to the Whiskey.

> "I'll go with you. Don't you want me to?" Dr. Sean McNamara asked.
> "After sex clinginess happens all the time - especially with older guys." Eden replied.
> "Are you saying there's no chemistry here?"
> "I like having sex with older men. It's a daddy thing. [But] I don't date guys with grey pubes."

Note the long title of this *Daily Mail* post: "Marilyn Monroe believed her lover Robert Kennedy would finally fill the void left by her absentee dad - after confessing how she wanted to 'put on a black wig, pick up her father in a bar and make love to him,' book [Charles Casillo's *Marilyn Monroe: The Private Life of a Public Icon*] reveals"

I must admit that some examples of the "daddy thing" were more shocking than others. For example, I wrote, per Nancy Friday's *My Secret Garden: Women's Sexual Fantasies*, that (some) lesbians have fantasies about having sex with men while they're having lesbian sex. Well, (some) lesbians use the "daddy thing" reference when being intimate. An example of this appeared on Amazon's *I Love Dick* (2017). During episode 3 of season 1, it was revealed that Toby (Bobbi Salvör Menuez), a young redheaded lipstick lesbian, was "touched" at an early age by her father, but that was after she began watching pornography. And during the episode, Toby visited Devon (Roberta Colindrez), a young butch lesbian, to apologize for getting Devon fired from the art gallery. And how did Toby apologize to Devon? She said, "I'm sorry daddy," before she got on her knees, unfastened Devon's jeans, and confessed, "I want to suck your big [strap-on] cock."

Of course, the "daddy thing" isn't restricted to United States. For instance, read the plot summary of *Puppylove* (2013) - a French coming of age film:

> At 14, Diane is an enigmatic teenager and a loner. She is busy bringing up her little brother, Marc, and has an intense relationship with her father, Christian. The appearance of Julia, a young charismatic and emancipated English girl, in her neighborhood turns Diane's everyday life upside down. Diane, who wants to break the bounds of childhood at any price, goes through the most dramatic experiences of her life in the space of six months. The closer she is to Julia, the more she turns her back on morality, paying no attention to the consequences or the limits of her desires.

In one scene, Diane's father barged into her room while she was taking a break from studying to watch pornography. After Diane refused to turn off the hardcore pornography, she politely asked her father to leave her room. Subsequently, in the very next scene, the nymphet masturbated in the bathtub. Below is Netflix's subtitles for the dialogue that took place between Diane and her father:

> Diane: You could knock.
>
> Father: What are you up to?
>
> Diane: I'm watching TV.
>
> Father: I came to say good night.
>
> Father: Switch that off.
>
> Diane: Good night.

In addition to the pornography and masturbation, the following erotic early teen behavior was exhibited by fourteen-year-old Diane in the French film:

1. She unsuccessfully attempted to have sex with another teen
2. She shared a lipstick lesbian kiss with Julia, her classmate, after Julia performed oral sex in the backseat of an older male's car
3. She defiantly ran topless into the shower - of the boy's locker room
4. She watched Julia have sex with the hotel's bartender while Julia's parents slept in the next hotel room

5. She sensuously kissed Julia in the hotel's bathroom

6. She performed oral sex on a man in a nightclub's bathroom

7. She and Julia had a three-way with a sailor in his cabin after commandeering his sailboat

But the parts of the film that are most relevant to this chapter are that Diane incestuously asked her father, "Could you make love to me?" And after Diane witnessed her father gazing upon a nude Julia and Julia stating about Diane's father, "I'm sure he likes youngsters.", Diane pulled back the shower curtain to give Julia a peep of her wet father. Subsequently, Julia kissed Diane's father, pulled down her white panties and, despite his resistance, seduced him into having sex against a tree.

Interestingly, *Puppylove* was directed and co-written by Delphine Lehericey, a female filmmaker, the film premiered at the San Sebastián International Film Festival, it won a Magritte Award for Best Original Score, and it was nominated for Best First Feature.

Before we end this chapter, let's take a look at the IMDb plot summaries for a Danish, Italian and another American film:

Daddy, Darling (1970): A young Danish girl (Helli Louise) seduces everything in sight after daddy (Ole Wisborg) refuses her naughty come-ons. She'll have a lesbian affair with her teacher, pretend that her teenage boyfriend is dear old dad and finally get to her stepmother (Gio Petre)

Mimi (1979) [Italian: Un dramma borghese]: The fifteen year-old Maria "Mimmina" Luiza leaves the boarding school in Genève to stay in the Bechten Hotel nursing her father, the widower writer Guido [...] Along the days, Guido recovers from his illness and Mimmina has a crush on him and tries to seduce her own father. When her roommate and best friend Therese [...] comes to the hotel to visit Mimmina, she has a love affair with Guido with tragic consequences.

Wicked (1998): 14-year-old Ellie Christianson (Julia Stiles) wants to make her father Ben her love partner. And when her mother Karen turns up dead, Ellie has a good opportunity.

Unsurprisingly, Franco isn't the only man who is being referred to as daddy on social media. For example, the Buzzfeed article "13 Really Hot Teachers That Will Have You Begging For Detention: Yes, Mr. Smith. I'll gladly stay after class," displays a number of photographs taken by high school girls of their "hot" teachers. The photographs were posted to Tumblr, Instagram, Snapchat and Twitter. "hot teachers, thank you for existing" was the caption on a Tumblr post of four "hot" male teachers. But the hashtags were more revealing than the pictures and captions: #Hot teachers, #teacherxstudent, #forbidden, #onesidedlove, #oldermen, #highschool. And of course: #DADDYAF and #FUXMEZADDYYYY.

Lastly, as I was working on this book, Halle Kiefer posted on *Vulture* "Dr. Phil Beseeches You to Please, Stop Commenting 'Daddy'." Kiefer wrote that Dr. Phil beseeched his young TikTok followers:

> "You have to stop commenting 'daddy' on all my posts […] I ain't your daddy. I hate to break it to you, but I ain't your daddy, and your real daddy is probably getting his feelings hurt. I appreciate the support. It's a little weird, but I do appreciate the support."

Thus, as you can see, those "daddy thing" comments that were posted on Franco's Instagram account are quite "normal".

Conclusion

We related previously, that per Ridley, research proves that all (heteronormative) men are nympholepts as they are attracted to a trinity of qualities: youth, figure, and face. And of course, James Franco is no different. However, as we stated, most men don't have high enough levels of self-confidence and self-esteem to initiate an affair with a nymphet – let alone marry a teen *à la* 50-year-old actor Doug Hutchison of *The X-Files* and *Lost* who married the buxom, blonde, and 16-year-old Courtney Stodden.

Yet, the easiest way to boost a passive nympholept's self-confident and self-esteem is for him to be propositioned by a nymphet, which is what happened to Anthony Weiner after the 15-year-old initiated a sexual relationship with him via Twitter. But Weiner's problem was that he wasn't in France where the age-of-consent is 15. And Weiner's rabbi may have frowned upon of Weiner's pre-marital sexting. Also, it should be no surprise that Franco attempted to arrange a (secular law-abiding) *rendezvous* with a Scottish nymphet. Without God Almighty's help, what mortal man could resist the temptation of (legally aged) nymphets prepositioning him with comments such as from slurpee.girrl: "Babe I am legal, u can fuck me n not get in trouble 4 it papi"

In addition, one should not be surprised that Franco's oeuvre, like that of Nabokov, Bukowski, and Henry Miller, is peppered with nympholepsy. But what is surprising is Franco's somewhat hypocritical attempt at criticizing Salinger for having an "obsession with innocence" when Franco's books, as we read, are liberally peppered with graphic pre-teen sex, graphic teen sex, and graphic age-gap sex. Yet, Franco did, possibly unintentionally, confirm Levine's assertions in her *Los Angeles Times* Book Prize winning tome that teens are sexual.

In the end, Franco, after his Instagram scandal, succumbed to the trolling of his age-gap relationship distractors; thus, unlike Charlie Chaplin and Woody Allen, Franco may never experience any "fun" as an actor slash director, which is unlike 45-year-old Leonardo DiCaprio, who per Daniella Scott of *Cosmopolitan* met Camila Morrone when she was 12, reunited with her when she was 19, and shortly thereafter started openly dating the baby faced actress.

Bibliography

Aadland, Florence. *The Beautiful Pervert.* Novel Books, 1965.

Abbott, Megan E. *The End of Everything: A Novel.* Back Bay Books, 2012.

Anderson, Christopher, et al. "The High Society That Surrounded Jeffrey Epstein." *Intelligencer,* New York Magazine, 22 July 2019, nymag.com/intelligencer/2019/07/jeffrey-epstein-high-society-contacts.html.

Anderson, Sam. "Is James Franco For Real? -- *New York Magazine* - Nymag." New York Magazine, 23 July 2010, nymag.com/movies/profiles/67284/.

Alexander, Paul. "J. D. Salinger's Women." New York Magazine, 9 Feb. 1998, nymag.com/nymetro/arts/features/2162/.'

"Alexis Neiers on Drugs, Prison, and the Bling Ring: Profiles by VICE." YouTube, Vice, 2014, www.youtube.com/watch?v=FH9-S6ntIBQ.

Allen, Woody. "Woody Allen Speaks Out." The New York Times, *The New York Times*, 8 Feb. 2014, www.nytimes.com/2014/02/09/opinion/sunday/woody-allen-speaks-out.html.

Baum, Gary. "Woody Allen's Secret Teen Lover Speaks: Sex, Power and a Conflicted Muse Who Inspired 'Manhattan'." *The Hollywood Reporter*, 19 Dec. 2018, www.hollywoodreporter.com/features/woody-allens-secret-teen-lover-manhattan-muse-speaks-1169782.

Blier, Bertrand, director. *Beau-Père.* Sara Films, 1981.

Bonaduce, Danny. *Random Acts of Badness: My Story.* Hyperion, 2001. www.imdb.com/title/tt0079077/?ref_=nv_sr_srsg_0.

Bors, Chris. "STEVE GIANAKOS: NEW PAINTINGS." *Artvoices Magazine*, Apr. 2012.

Carvalho, Claudio. *Mimi.* IMDb, IMDb.com, 31 Aug. 1979

Casillo, Charles. *Marilyn Monroe: The Private Life of a Public Icon.* Griffin, 2018.

Chaplin, Lita Grey, and Morton Cooper. *My Life with Chaplin: An Intimate Memoir.* Dell Pub., 1966.

Crowe, Cameron. Ridgemont High: A True Story. Simon and Schuster, 1981.

"Daddy, Darling." *IMDb*, IMDb.com, 12 Feb. 1971,
www.imdb.com/title/tt0062847/?ref_=nv_sr_srsg_0.

Dean, Alexandra, director. *This Is Paris*. YouTube, 14 Sept. 2020,
www.youtube.com/watch?v=wOg0TY1jG3w&t=2
341s.

DeLappe, Sarah. *The Wolves: A Play*. The Overlook Press,
2018.

Dennen, Barry. *My Life with Barbra: A Love Story*. Prometheus
Books, 1997.

Duggan, Katie. "The Women of the Woody Allen Archives."
Nassau Weekly, 23 Apr. 2019,
nassauweekly.com/the-women-
of-the-woody-allen-archives/.

Editors, The. "Who Was Jeffrey Epstein Calling? A Close Study of
His Circle — Social, Professional, Transactional —
Reveals a Damning Portrait of Elite New York."
Intelligencer, 22 July 2019, nymag.com/intelligencer
/amp/2019/07/jeffrey-epstein-high-society-
contacts.html.

Eells, Josh. "Inside 'Spring Breakers,' the Most Debauched Movie
of the Year." *Rolling Stone*, 25 June 2018,
www.rollingstone.com/movies/movie-news/inside-
spring- breakers-the-most-debauched
-movie-of-the-year-184469/.

Finstad, Suzanne. *Child Bride: The Untold Story of Priscilla
Beaulieu Presley*. Three Rivers Press, 2005.

Fox, James. "Roman 'Holiday'" *Vanity Fair*, Oct. 2013,
archive.vanityfair.com/article/2013/10/roman-holiday.

Franco, James. *Actors Anonymous: A Novel*. Little A, 2013.

Franco, James. *A California Childhood*. Insight, 2013.

Franco, James. Bungalow 89 - A Short Story by James Franco, *Vice*,
2014, www.vice.com/en/article/ppm379/bungalow-89-
0000347-v21n6.

Franco, James. *Directing Herbert White*: Poems. Graywolf
Press, 2014.

Franco, James. *Hollywood Dreaming: Stories, Pictures, and Poems*.
Insight Editions, 2014.

Franco, James. "J. D. Salinger's War." VICE, 11 Oct. 2013,
www.vice.com/sv/article/exm4jm/j-d-salingers-war.

Franco, James. *Palo Alto Stories*. Eichborn, 2012.

Franco, James. *Straight James/Gay James*. Hansen Publishing Group,
Llc, 2015.

Franco, James. *Strongest of the Litter: A Chapbook*. Hollyridge Press, 2012.

Franco, James. "The Meanings of the Selfie." *The New York Times*, 26 Dec. 2013, www.nytimes.com/2013/12/29/arts/the-meanings-of-the-selfie.html?auth=link-dismiss-google1tap.

Friday, Nancy. *My Secret Garden: Women's Sexual Fantasies*. Pocket Books, 1974.

Gardner, Howard. *Creating Minds: an Anatomy of Creativity Seen through the Lives of Freud, Einstein, Picasso, Stravinsky, Eliot, Graham, and Gandhi*. Basic Books, 1994.

Galindo, Brian. "13 Really Hot Teachers That Will Have You Begging For Detention." *BuzzFeed*, 19 Jan. 1970, www.buzzfeed.com/mjs538/mmmmmmmm.

Gardner, Eriq. "James Franco Settles Lawsuit Over Charles Bukowski Biopic." *The Hollywood Reporter*, 7 May 2020, www.hollywoodreporter.com/thr-esq/james-franco-settles-lawsuit-charles-745235.

Gardner, Howard E. *Creating Minds An Anatomy of Creativity Seen Through the Lives of Freud, Einstein, Picasso, Stravinsky, Eliot, Graham, and Ghandi*. Basic Books, 1993.

Geimer, Samantha. "Exclusive: Polanski Victim Blames Media." ABC News, ABC News Network, 2011, abcnews.go.com/GMA/video/exclusive-roman-polanski-victim-blames-media-13103307.

Gelman, Brett. "Santa Daddy." *Vice*, 31 Dec. 2012, www.vice.com/en_us/article/znq59e/combover-santa-daddy-0000345-v19n12.

Giorgi Moshe. "James Franco on LIVE with Kelly and Michael." Online video clip. YouTube, April 7, 2014. Web, April 22, 2020.

Goodman, Alana. "Anthony Weiner Carried on a Months-Long Online Sexual Relationship with a 15-Year-Old Girl." *Daily Mail Online*, Associated Newspapers, 21 Sept. 2016, www.dailymail.co.uk/news/article-3790824/Anthony-Weiner-carried-months-long-online-sexual-relationship-troubled-15-year-old-girl-telling-hard-asking-dress-school-girl-outfits-pressing-engage-rape-fantasies.html?ito=social-twitter_dailymailus.

Green, David Gordon, director. *Pineapple Express*. Sony Pictures, 2008.

Griffith, Keith. "James Franco's Creepy Musings on Sex with
        'Young Girls'." *Daily Mail Online*, Associated
        Newspapers, 15 Jan. 2018, www.dailymail.co.uk
        /news/article-5265135/James-Francos-
        creepy-musings-sex-young-girls.html.

Hamri, Sanaa. *Shameless*, Season 1, episode 11, Showtime, 20
        Mar. 2011.

Heckerling, Amy, director. *Fast Times at Ridgemont High*. 1982.

Howe, Caroline. "How Marilyn Monroe Looked for Her Absent
        Father in Robert Kennedy." Daily Mail Online, Associated
        Newspapers, 17 Aug. 2018, www.dailymail.co.uk/
        news/article-6064857/How-Marilyn-Monroe-looked-
        absent-father-Robert-Kennedy.html.

Howley, Malka. "You Know You Like Little Girls: Lana Del
        Rey and Dolores Haze." *PopMatters*, 16 Aug. 2018,
        www.popmatters.com/lana-del-rey-dolores-haze-
        2495787697.html.

Ibrahim, Mo. "CYBORG 2: Nude Teen Angelina Jolie in
        Age-Gap Sex Scene." *The Allure of Nymphets*, 30
        Mar. 2020, www.theallureofnymphets.com/2020/03/
        cyborg-2-nude-teen-angelina-jolie-in.html.

Ibrahim, Mo. *Nymphalis Carmen: Nympholepsy in Nabokov's
        Oeuvre*. Lad Literature, 2017.

Ibrahim, Mo. Teen Paris Hilton in Push Up Bra: "You Derty Lil
        Girl" & Paris' Teen Age-Gap Sex Tape, 1 Jan. 1970,
        www.theallureofnymphets.com/2020/04/teen-paris-
        hilton-in-push-up-bra-you.html.

Ibrahim, Mo. *The Allure of Nymphets: From Emperor Augustus
        to Woody Allen, A Study of Man's Fascination with Very Young
        Women*. 2nd ed., Lad Literature, 2017.

Ibsen, Henrik. *Ghosts*. Astounding Stories, 2017.

Insatiable. Netflix, created by Lauren Gussis, season 1,
        Netflix, 2018.

Intimacy. By Thomas Bradshaw, directed by Scott Elliott, N.D.,
        Acorn Theatre, New York, NY.

Jung, E. Alex. "How Does the New It Movie Deal With
        Stephen King's Orgy Scene?" *Vulture*, 8 Sept. 2017,
        www.vulture.com/2017/09/how-the-new-
        it-movie-deals-with-the-child-orgy-scene.html.

K, Michael. "James Franco Tried To Pick Up A 17-Year-Old
        On Instagram." Dlisted, 3 Apr. 2014,

dlisted.com/2014/04/02/james-franco-mightve-tried-to-pick-up-a-17-year-old-on-instagram/.

Kiefer, Halle. *Dr. Phil Beseeches You to Please, Stop Commenting 'Daddy' on All His Posts*. Vulture, 12 Sept. 2020, www.vulture.com/2020/09/dr-phil-posts-tiktok-asking-fans-to-stop-commenting-daddy.html.

Kashner, Sam. "Dangerous Talents." *Vanity Fair*, 10 Oct. 2006, www.vanityfair.com/news/2005/03/rebel200503.

Koppelman, Brian, director. *Solitary Man*. Millennium Films, 2009.

Lambe, Stacy. "EXCLUSIVE: First Look at James Franco Revision of Tori Spelling's 'Mother, May I Sleep With Danger?'." Wfaa.com, WFAA, 20 May 2016, www.wfaa.com/article/entertainment/entertainment-tonight/exclusive-first-look-at-james-franco-revision-of-tori-spellings-mother-may-i-sleep-with-danger/287-207493021.

Lawson, Richard. "*Pretty Wild* Might Be the Worst Television Show Ever Made." *Gawker*, 29 Mar. 2010, gawker.com/5504679/pretty-wild-might-be-the-worst-television-show-ever-made.

Lehericey, Delphine, director. *Puppylove*. Entre Chien Et Loup Liaison, 2013.

Leigh, Spencer. "Dory Previn: Singer and Songwriter Hailed for Hersearing Honesty." *The Independent*, Independent Digital News and Media, 15 Feb. 2012, www.independent.co.uk/news/obituaries/dory-previn-singer-and-songwriter-hailed-for-hersearing-honesty-6945652.html.

Lewis, Andy. "Roman Polanski Rape Victim Unveils Startling, Disturbing Photo for Book Cover (Exclusive)." *The Hollywood Reporter*, 25 July 2013, www.hollywoodreporter.com/news/roman-polanski-rape-victim-unveils-591015.

Leonard, Tom. "Liz Taylor at 16 Had ALREADY Been Seduced by Mickey Rooney, Ronald Reagan, Errol Flynn and JFK." *Daily Mail Online*, Associated Newspapers, 17 Oct. 2015, www.dailymail.co.uk/femail/article-3276713/This-Liz-Taylor-16-seduced-half-Hollywood-Mickey-Rooney-Ronald-Reagan-Errol-Flynn-threesome-JFK-new-book-raises-extraordinary-questions.html.

Maheshwari, Sapna. "American Apparel Reveals X-Rated Alleged

Messages Between Founder And Staff."
BuzzFeed News, 23 June 2015, www.buzzfeednews
.com/article/sapna/american-apparel-reveals-
raunchy-messages-between-ex-ceo-and#.ts
D0507vR.

Milton, Joyce. *Tramp: The Life of Charlie Chaplin*. Da Capo Press,
1998.

Mont, Jane, art. *My Ideal Bookshelf*. Edited by Thessaly La
Force, Little, Brown and Company, 2012.

Nash, Alanna. *Baby, Let's Play House: Elvis Presley and the
Women Who Loved Him*. HarperCollins, 2010.

Nabokov, Vladimir. *Pale Fire*. Vintage, 1989.

Petersen, Anne Helen. *Scandals of Classic Hollywood: Sex,
Deviance, and Drama from the Golden Age of American Cinema*.
Center Point Large Print, 2015.

Porter, Darwin, and Danforth Prince. *Elizabeth Taylor: There
Is Nothing Like a Dame*. Blood Moon, 2012.

Mamet, David. *Sexual Perversity in Chicago and The Duck
Variations*. Grove Press, 1978.

Mann, William J. *Hello, Gorgeous: Becoming Barbra Streisand*.
Houghton Mifflin Harcourt, 2013.

Maynard, Joyce. *At Home in the World: A Memoir*. Picador USA,
2013.

Mathews, Nancy Mowll. *Paul Gauguin: An Erotic Life*. Yale
University Press, 2001.

McGillicuddy, Larry. *Wicked*. IMDb, IMDb.com, 17 Jan.
1998, www.imdb.com/title/tt0120088/
?ref_=nv_sr_srsg_0.

Merkin, Daphne, et al. "After Decades of Silence, Soon-Yi
Previn Speaks." *Vulture*, New York Magazine, 17 Sept.
2018, www.vulture.com/2018/09/
soon-yi-previn-speaks.html.

Morgan, Richard. "Perspective | I Read Decades of Woody
Allen's Private Notes. He's Obsessed with Teenage
Girls." *The Washington Post*, WP Company, 4 Jan. 2018,
www.washingtonpost.com/outlook/
i-read-decades-of-woody-allens-private-notes-hes-
obsessed-with-teenage-girls/2018/01/04/f2701482-
f03b-11e7-b3bf-
ab90a706e175_story.html?noredirect=on.

McGuire, Patrick. "Cowards Are Blackmailing Young Women

to Death on the Internet." *Vice*, 21 Dec. 2012,
www.vice.com/en_us/article/xd4pk7/cowards-are-
blackmailing-young-women-to-death-on-the-internet-
0000556-v19n12.

Nabokov, Vladimir Vladimirovich, and Alfred Appel. *The
Annotated Lolita*. London: Penguin, 2000.

O'Connor, Maureen. "Pornhub Is the Kinsey Report of Our
Time." *The Cut*, New York Magazine, 12 June 2017,
www.thecut.com/2017/06/pornhub-and-the-american
-sexual-imagination.html.

Odem, Mary E. *Delinquent Daughters: Protecting and Policing
Adolescent Female Sexuality in the United States, 1885-1920*.
The University of North Carolina Press, 2000.

Orth , Maureen. "Mia Farrow's Story: On Frank Sinatra,
Battling Scandal, and Raising Her Family." *Vanity Fair*,
23 Oct. 2013, www.vanityfair.com/style/
2013/11/mia-farrow-frank-sinatra-ronan-farrow.

Porter, Darwin, and Danforth Prince. *Elizabeth Taylor: There
Is Nothing Like a Dame*. Blood Moon, 2012.

Potts , Kim. "'127' Facts About James Franco." *Moviefone*, 2 Nov.
2010, blog.moviefone.com/2010/
11/02/james-franco-facts.

Roberts, Glenys. "New Film on How Chateau Marmont
Became a Byword for Hollywood Debauchery." *Daily
Mail Online*, Associated Newspapers, 27 Nov. 2010,
www.dailymail.co.uk/tvshowbiz/article-1333487/New
film-Chateau-Marmont-byword-Hollywood-debauche.
Html.

Rose Spiegel, Amy, et al. "Older Men." *Rookie*, 22 Apr. 2013,
www.rookiemag.com/2013/01/older-men/.

Rice, Anne. *Belinda*. Jove Books, 2014.

Ridley, Matt. *The Red Queen: Sex and the Evolution of
Human Nature*. Verlag Nicht Ermittelbar, 2003.

Salerno, Shane, director. *Salinger*. The Story Factory, 2013.

Setoodeh, Ramin. "James Franco on 'The Disaster Artist' and
How He Conquered His Fear of Failure." *Variety*, Variety,
14 Nov. 2017, variety.com/2017/film/news/
james-franco-the-disaster-artist-the-deuce-1202613750/.

"Scenes from a Marriage." Arnold, Andrea, director. *I Love
Dick*, season 1, episode 3, 2017, Amazon.

Scherstuhl, Alan. "Salinger Would Make Holden Caulfield

Puke." The Village Voice, 4 Sept. 2013,
www.villagevoice.com/2013/09/04/salinger-would-
make-holden-caulfield-puke/.

Schwartz, Ben. "The Double Life of Peter Arno, The New
Yorker's Most Influential Cartoonist." Vanity Fair, 5 Apr.
2016, www.vanityfair.com/culture/2016/
04/peter-arno-the-new-yorker-cartoonist.

Scott, Daniella. "Leo DiCaprio and Girlfriend Camila Morrone Just
Made Their First Public Appearance at the Oscars."
Cosmopolitan, 13 Feb. 2020, www.cosmopolitan.com/
uk/entertainment/a30845732/leonardo-dicaprio-camila-
morrone-girlfriend-first-public-appearance-oscars/.

Stern, Howard. "Show Rundown: April 7, 2011." *Howard Stern*,
7 Apr. 2011,
www.howardstern.com/show/2011/4/7/stacey-nelkin-
actress-sexpert-rundownshow-302/.

Taraborrelli, J. Randy. *Sinatra: Behind the Legend.*
Pan Books, 2016.

Tonita Queta Parks. "Howard Stern's speaks out about
Instagram Scandal" Online video clip. YouTube, April 30,
2014. Web. April 21, 2020.

Waldman, Adelle. In This Novel, a Secret Society Is Keeping Some
Very Dark Secrets. *The New York Times*, 16 Apr. 2019,
www.nytimes.com/2019/04/16/books/review/club-
takis-wurger.html.

Weiner, Jonah. "The Mystery of James Franco: Inside His
Manic Days and Sleepless Nights." Rolling Stone, 25
June 2018, www.rollingstone.com/tv/tv-news/
The-mystery-of-james-franco-inside-his-manic-days-
and-sleepless-nights-117022/.

Zenovich, Marina, director. *Roman Polanski: Odd Man Out.*
Perfect Weekend, 2012.

Books by Mo Ibrahim

Nymphalis carmen: Nympholepsy in Nabokov's Oeuvre

Katie: A Novella

*The Allure of Nymphets: From Emperor Augustus to Woody Allen, A Study
of Man's Fascination with Very Young Women*

The Rubber Room: A Novel Account from New York City's Teacher Jail

www.TheWriterMoIbrahim.com

www.TheAllureofNymphets.com

www.ingramcontent.com/pod-product-compliance
Lightning Source LLC
Chambersburg PA
CBHW051055250726
48656CB00001B/306